COST OF LIVING STUDIES. V

HOW MEXICANS EARN AND LIVE

A STUDY OF THE INCOMES AND EXPENDITURES
OF ONE HUNDRED MEXICAN FAMILIES
IN SAN DIEGO, CALIFORNIA

BY

THE HELLER COMMITTEE FOR RESEARCH IN SOCIAL ECONOMICS
OF THE UNIVERSITY OF CALIFORNIA

AND

CONSTANTINE PANUNZIO

Reprinted with the permission of The Regents of the University of California

JOHNSON REPRINT CORPORATION
Fifth Avenue, New York, N.Y. 10003

JOHNSON REPRINT COMPANY LTD.
Berkeley Square House, London, W. 1

University of California Publications in Economics
Volume 13, No. 1, pp. 1–114
Issued May 17, 1933

University of California Press
Berkeley, California

———

Cambridge University Press
London, England

First reprinting, 1966, Johnson Reprint Corporation
Printed in the United States of America

THE HELLER COMMITTEE FOR RESEARCH IN SOCIAL ECONOMICS

CONTENTS

		PAGE
Foreword		vii
Acknowledgments		ix
I.	Introductory	1
II.	Social data	7
III.	Income	14
IV.	Expenditure	28
V.	Expenditure (*concluded*)	49
VI.	Summary	66
VII.	Comparison with other cost of living studies	68
VIII.	Case histories	92

APPENDICES

A. Clothing details 109
B. Average expenditure per family for specified items regardless of the number of families reporting such expenditures . 114

LIST OF TABLES

	PAGE
1. Composition of household	7
2. Birthplace of members of the families	8
3. Age of husbands and wives	8
4. Number of children living at home per family	9
5. Age of children at last birthday	10
6. Occupations of men and women	12
7. Amount of total family income during the year	14
8. Amount and percentage of annual income from specified sources	15
9. Amount of man's earnings during the year	16
10. Status of dependency of children, classified by age	18
11. Total annual expenditure per consumption unit	25
12. Surpluses and deficits reported at close of year	26
13. Amount and percentage of annual expenditure for the main items of the family budget	29

LIST OF TABLES—(*Continued*)

PAGE

14. Comparative distribution of average weekly food expenditure . . 31
15. Expenditure for food per equivalent adult male unit 34
16. Number of families reporting a specified expenditure for clothing, and the number of such families receiving gifts of clothing within the year 36
17. Expenditure for housing according to conditions of tenure . . . 39
18. Number of rooms classified by size of household 41
19. Expenditure for items of house operation 44
20. Expenditure during the year for furniture and furnishings . . . 47
21. Expenditure for care of the person 48
22. Expenditure for leisure-time activities 50
23. Expenditure for automobiles 53
24. Expenditure for transportation 54
25. Expenditure for investments during the year 56
26. Expenditure for medical care 59
27. Expenditure for association dues 61
28. Expenditure for educational items 62
29. Expenditure for charity 63
30. Expenditure for specified residual items 64
31. Percentage distribution of expenditures by New York workingmen's families—Chapin, 1907—compared with Mexicans 70
32. Percentage distribution of expenditures by Homestead mill hands—Byington, 1907-8—compared with Mexicans 74
33. Percentage distribution of expenditures by wage-earners' families in the United States—United States Bureau of Labor Statistics, 1918-19 —compared with Mexicans 76
34. Average (mean) expenditure per family reporting for certain significant items by wage-earners' families in the United States—United States Bureau of Labor Statistics, 1918-19—compared with Mexicans 77
35. Average expenditure per family regardless of the number reporting and percentage distribution of expenditure by Oakland street-car men—Heller Committee, 1924-25—compared with Mexicans . . . 80
36. Average (mean) expenditure per family reporting for certain significant items by Oakland street-car men—Heller Committee, 1924-25—compared with Mexicans 81
37. Average expenditure per family regardless of the number reporting and percentage distribution of expenditure by Ford employees in Detroit—United States Bureau of Labor Statistics, 1929—compared with Mexicans 85
38. Percentage distribution of expenditures by Mexican government employees, 1930, compared with San Diego Mexicans 89

FOREWORD

THE STUDY HEREWITH PRESENTED, though primarily a cost of living study, is perhaps most interesting if regarded as a study in national adjustment.

According to current ways of thinking, the principle of nationalism is one of the fundamental guides to life. Every nation has its particular form of nationalism, and strangers coming to a new land are today inevitably called on to adjust themselves to the forms of life that taken together constitute the "nationalism" they find about them.

The adjustment may result from a desire on the part of the immigrant to fit in, or from insistence on the part of those who are living according to the national standards. The motive is not here in question. The point is that immigrants must and do adjust.

Such an adjustment is plainly evident in this study of one hundred Mexican families. According to those who have been in Mexico, Mexican ways of living, especially those of the mass of the working class, differ greatly from the ways of living in the United States. Whether they differ to the advantage of the Mexican or to that of the American living in the United States depends on the point of view of the investigator. The one consideration here is the fact of difference. These one hundred families, whose earnings and spendings are given in detail, show the habits of living of a group not yet wholly adjusted to the American standard. The food consumption of these families still tends to resemble strongly that of the land from which they came. As to the use of other forms of consumer's goods, each category plainly shows the families being subjected in varying degrees to the new conditions of economic life in which they find themselves.

Because Mexicans are among our latest comers, and because they are a source of special interest in that they are late comers, the cost of living study contained in the ensuing pages should mean a contribution to more than facts about the cost of living. In addition, it pictures the ways of living of a national group of recent arrivals. It is hoped that those who study the tables, which give plainly and exactly what these families earned and how they spent what they earned, will also find less specifically set forth certain facts that will help tell a story of the adjustments that take place as new peoples come slowly but surely under the influence of our national life.

JESSICA B. PEIXOTTO, *Chairman,*
Heller Committee for Research in Social Economics

BERKELEY, CALIFORNIA

ACKNOWLEDGMENTS

THE AUTHORS of this study have many acknowledgments to make. Through the good offices of Dr. Paul S. Taylor, of the University of California, Professor Panunzio and the Heller Committee were enabled to plan and carry out the study as a joint undertaking. The Board of Directors of San Diego Neighborhood House made it possible for Professor Panunzio, then Director of the House, to take charge of the investigation and for the staff to conduct the actual field work. In addition, the Board of Directors contributed about one-half the cost of the field work. The rest was contributed by Professor and Mrs. Panunzio. Acknowledgment is due also to the Board of Education of the San Diego City Schools, and in particular to Superintendent Walter S. Hepner, who made the services of some of the Immigrant Education teachers available for the field work. Mrs. Lenore Panunzio, at that time Supervisor of Immigrant Education for the city schools, secured this cooperation. Special mention should be made of Miss Marian Branson, home teacher in the city schools, and Mrs. Grace Jacques, a member of the staff at Neighborhood House, who did the major part of the field work. The patience and skill of the investigators and the cheerful cooperation of the Mexican families themselves in the face of a prolonged and tedious inquiry deserve grateful mention.

The preparation of this study has been shared between the joint authors. The study was initiated and the field investigation in San Diego was directed by Professor Panunzio. The schedule and technique of the study were adapted from the form used by the Heller Committee in earlier investigations. The Heller Committee analyzed the findings and, in collaboration with Professor Panunzio, has prepared them for publication.

HOW MEXICANS EARN AND LIVE

A STUDY OF THE INCOMES AND EXPENDITURES OF ONE HUNDRED MEXICAN FAMILIES IN SAN DIEGO, CALIFORNIA

BY

THE HELLER COMMITTEE FOR RESEARCH IN SOCIAL ECONOMICS
OF THE UNIVERSITY OF CALIFORNIA
AND
CONSTANTINE PANUNZIO

I

INTRODUCTORY

FOR THE PAST THREE OR FOUR DECADES, Mexican immigration to the United States has brought out two sharply contrasted views concerning the Mexican. On the one hand, the Mexican's racial and cultural background, his capacity for work, his standard of living, his adaptability to our institutions have all been subjected to hostile criticism. On the other hand, he has been acclaimed as an admirable and competent addition to the low-scale wage group regarded as an integral part of economic progress. The group that criticizes makes itself very audible. Organized labor opposes the Mexican chiefly as a competitor of the American laborer. He is accused of a tendency to take wages below the minimum standard set by trade unions. Social workers for the most part see in the Mexicans an addition to the population which adds large numbers to the indigents in any community where they settle. Employers look at the matter differently. For them the Mexican is a necessary adjunct of the present labor supply in the United States. His are the hands which are ready to do the spade work.

Both points of view are based on armchair observations or practical day-to-day experience, rather than on studies of facts. Since 1929 a series of ordered observations has been published, adding facts to these opinions. Of first importance are the field studies of Dr. Paul S. Taylor of the University of California, nine monographs (1929–1933) on *Mexican Labor in the United States.* This series of investigations gives many and valuable data about the life and labor of the Mexican. The scholarly detachment that characterizes the presentation of the material adds weight and conviction. Governor C. C. Young's Fact-Finding Committee's Report, *Mexicans in California* (1930), is another source of new information. Two studies by Dr. Manuel Gamio, *Mexican Immigration to the United States* (1930) and *The Mexican Immigrant* (1931), also help to throw light on certain major aspects in the life of the Mexican. Together these studies answer questions such as the following: Are the Mexicans actually needed as laborers? Do they receive wages commensurate with the work they do in a given community? Are the wages they receive adequate to meet their cost of living? Are they, relatively speaking, a good social element in the community?

The study contained in the following pages answers those questions particularly relating to the cost of living. A detailed picture is given of the ways of spending of one hundred Mexican nonmigratory, wage-earning families residing in a Mexican neighborhood in 1929–1930. Whether the group is typical is matter for question. The families studied lived in the city of San Diego. They are a sample of the Mexican wage-earning population of California. To say that they are a typical and representative sample of the Mexican wage-earning group in the United States or in the State would be to add a guess to certainties.

A few facts concerning the Mexican population in California may give the group a further statistical setting. The restrictive immigration laws of 1921 and 1924, greatly reducing as they did the supply of low-skilled labor from southern and eastern Europe, brought in the Mexican, who was unaffected by these laws. The proportion of Mexicans in the total immigration into the United States rose from 3.8 per cent in the fiscal years 1911–1921 to 18.8 per cent in the year ended June 30, 1928.[1] In 1930 there were 1,422,533 Mexicans in the United States.[2] Because of the change in classification it is impossible to make a direct comparison with the number reported in 1920, but it seems fair to estimate the increase in the number of Mexicans in these ten years as more than 100 per cent, whereas the total population of the United States increased only 16 per cent in this period. In 1930, Mexicans constituted 1.2 per cent of the total population of the United States; of this number, 26 per cent were in California. Census figures show that there were 368,013 Mexicans in California, constituting 6.5 per cent of the State's total population. Within the State the major part of the Mexicans were concentrated in the ten southern counties of Imperial, Kern, Los Angeles, Orange, Riverside, Santa Barbara, San Bernardino, San Diego, San Luis Obispo, and Ventura. In 1930 these counties had a population of 3,044,978, or 53.6 per cent of the total population of the State. In this population were 291,401 Mexicans, 79.2 per cent of all the Mexicans in California. The average proportion of Mexicans to total population in these ten counties was 9.6 per cent. In Imperial County it rose to 35 per cent, in Ventura to 25 per cent. The Mexicans are more concentrated in the rural districts than in large cities. In California cities of 25,000 and over, the proportion of Mexicans to total population in 1930 was 5.4 per cent; in the remainder of the State it was 7.8 per cent. Recent years have shown a tendency for Mexicans to move into the cities,[3] but 52.5 per cent of the Mexicans in California in 1930 were in rural districts or towns of less than 25,000 population.

The facts of population had very little to do with the choice of San Diego as the location for the study herewith presented. Rather, the city was chosen because Professor Panunzio was at that time Director of San Diego Neighborhood House, a philanthropic enterprise in the Mexican district. The group of families included in this study was not, therefore, necessarily typical of the average Mexican family in California. These families were residents of one of the five

---

[1] *Mexicans in California*, 19–20. This figure includes only those legally admitted.
[2] Fifteenth Census of the United States (1930).
[3] *Mexicans in California*, 57.

cities in the State with more than 100,000 population. Thus, automatically, all agricultural and migratory workers were excluded from the study. In 1930, 2.5 per cent of all Mexicans in California lived in San Diego, whose total population of 147,995 contained 9,266 Mexicans, 6.3 per cent of the population.

Mexicans live in San Diego under conditions that are, possibly, more than usually favorable. Most of them are in the southwestern portion of the city along the waterfront close to the factories and canneries. The streets are wide; sanitation is moderately good. Mexican stores, churches, pool halls, and the Neighborhood House are a part of the district. Living conditions are reasonably good. There is little or no serious congestion. The cottage type of house prevails. There are no slum tenements.

As Dr. Gamio has pointed out,[4] the mode of living of the Mexican workman who has become a resident of the United States naturally changes. If the following study is of value, it will show, first, the detail of this divergence between the Mexican's standard of living in this country and his standard of living at home, and, secondly, the divergence between the Mexican immigrant standard and the American standard. Mexicans on the whole retain the food habits of their own country, but they tend to adopt American clothing, and their housing conditions show a great improvement over those prevailing in Mexico.

The data presented in the following study, then, represent a sample of the Mexican settled in a moderately large city in California, who as a wage earner or small tradesman is adjusting himself with a larger income to a way of spending which is partly that which he brought from his own land and partly that of the land in which he lives.

In order that the group of families studied should be as homogeneous as possible, certain qualifications were set up: (1) One of the parents must be Mexican.[5] (2) The family must have been

---

[4] *Mexican immigration to the United States*, 140–147.

[5] In the Census of 1930 persons of Mexican birth or parentage who were not definitely returned as white or Indian were designated "Mexican." The same rule has been followed in the present study, so that "Mexican" implies race and not birthplace.

resident in San Diego for the twelve months preceding the investigation. (3) Both parents must be alive and at home. (4) The family must include at least one child.

As is usual in such studies, the families were in the main self-supporting and independent. Families were included, however, which received free medical care—the almost universal resource of the low-paid wage earner, gifts of clothing from an organization like the Parent-Teachers' Association, or milk free or at reduced rates from a milk station.

The study was designed to comprise only wage earners in the strict sense of the term; but the investigators included families of similar social and economic status in which the man was the proprietor of a small business, earning no more than the average skilled laborer, or a salaried clerk. The final group may, therefore, be more truly described as the "low-income" class than as the "wage-earning" class.

The information collected from these families included full details about source and amount of income, items of expenditure, and surplus or deficit, of the preceding twelve months. In addition, certain special and identifying data were gathered, concerning housing conditions, and the degree of dependency, age, sex, and birthplace of every member of the household.[6]

The information was gathered in the summer of 1930. The investigators were members of the staff of Neighborhood House, San Diego, of which Professor Panunzio was then Director, and teachers of adult classes in English in the city school system. The families visited were either personally known to the investigator or were neighbors or relatives of families already included.

As has been said, the final study explains the way of living of 100 families. Twenty-two additional schedules were discarded, usually because of an unexplained discrepancy greater than 10 per cent between income and expenditure; occasionally because a family was obviously of a higher economic level, or because of

---

[6] A similar schedule was published in a previous Heller Committee report, *Spending ways of a semi-skilled group,* University of California Publications in Economics, 5 (1931): 295–366. Copies of the schedule used in the present study may be obtained from the Heller Committee.

refusal to give certain necessary information. The resources available for field work and compilation set the limit at 100 completed schedules. Statistically, this should be an adequate sample of a fairly homogeneous group.

Within the limits of the qualifications just noted, every attempt was made to secure an unbiased sample. Of course, in all studies of this kind the voluntary self-selection of the families which were willing to cooperate and the difficulties of recalling details of income and expenditure with the requisite accuracy are likely to single out the more intelligent and thrifty.

II

SOCIAL DATA

Composition of household.—The character of the group was determined by the qualifications set up for inclusion in the study. Thus there were a husband and a wife in each family, and at least one child. The average family had between three and four children. In a few families there were other relatives; two households included lodgers.[7]

TABLE 1

COMPOSITION OF HOUSEHOLD*

Members of household	Total number of persons in the group		Number of families containing such persons
All persons..................................	600		100
Members of family*......................	558		100
Husbands†..............................		100	100
Wives.....................................		100	100
Children.................................		358	100
Relatives...................................	40		27
Lodgers.....................................	2		2

* "Family" includes only parents and children. "Household" includes all members of family, all relatives living in the house, and lodgers.
† Two of these husbands were working away from home at the end of the study.

Nativity.—Ninety-one per cent of the parents and only 28 per cent of the children were natives of Mexico. Of the 271 persons born in the United States, all but two were born in California or the Southwest, the great majority in the former. Sixteen families included one American-born parent; ninety-one had at least one American-born child, and in over half the families all the children were born in the United States.

---

[7] Composition of household, ages, and housing conditions are reported for the date of the investigator's visit, ignoring variations at other periods of the year.

TABLE 2

BIRTHPLACE OF MEMBERS OF THE FAMILIES

Country of birth	All persons in family		Parents				Children	
			Fathers		Mothers			
	Number	Percentage	Number	Percentage	Number	Percentage	Number	Percentage
Total............................	558	....	100	....	100	....	358	....
Not reported..............	10	....	2	....	2	....	6	....
Total reported............	548	100.0	98	100.0	98	100.0	352	100.0
Born in United States	271	49.5	6	6.1	12	12.2	253	71.9
Born in Mexico..........	277	50.5	92	93.9	86	87.8	99	28.1

Age of husbands and wives.—The requirement that each family should contain one child living at home limited the group so that

TABLE 3

AGE OF HUSBANDS AND WIVES

Age	Husbands		Wives	
	Number	Percentage	Number	Percentage
All ages............................	100	....	100	....
Not reported..................	1	....	1	....
Total reported..............	99	100.0	99	100.0
20–24................................	2	2.0	15	15.2
25–29................................	17	17.2	25	25.3
30–34................................	15	15.2	20	20.2
35–39................................	17	17.2	19	19.2
40–44................................	17	17.2	12	12.1
45–49................................	22	22.2	5	5.0
50–54................................	4	4.0	2	2.0
55–59................................	4	4.0	1	1.0
60–64................................	1	1.0	....	....
Average				
Mean................................	38.9 years		32.8 years	
Median............................	38.0 years		31.0 years	

few of the parents were either very young or elderly. Very few of the men were under twenty-five years of age, or over fifty. Nearly half the wives were between twenty-five and thirty-five; few were over forty-five.

Children at home.—The 100 families had 358 children living at home at the time of the investigation.[8] Nearly half the families had either three or four children; only four families had more than six. Exactly half the children were boys.

TABLE 4

NUMBER OF CHILDREN LIVING AT HOME PER FAMILY

Number of children	Number of families having specified number of children	
	All children	Dependent and semi-dependent* children
Total	100	100
None	....	....
One	16	16
Two	14	16
Three	20	22
Four	22	22
Five	12	11
Six	12	10
Seven	1	1
Eight	1	1
Nine	1	....
Ten	1	1
Average		
Mean	3.6	3.4
Median	3.5	3.3

* That is, earning less than 85 per cent of their cost of maintenance.

Most of the children were of school age or younger. Thirty-eight per cent were less than six years old. Nearly three-fourths were under eleven, and only 10 per cent were sixteen years or older. Of

---

[8] Children living away from home are not included in this study.

the latter group, only six—two boys and four girls—were over twenty-one. The typical family was thus composed of young children, dependent on the father's earnings. Only one family in five had a child old enough to be legally self-supporting, and these were generally the larger families with an unusual number of younger children.

TABLE 5

AGE OF CHILDREN AT LAST BIRTHDAY

Age	Number	Percentage
All ages	358	100.0
Less than 6	135	37.7
6–10	118	33.0
11–15	70	19.5
16–20	29	8.1
21 and over	6	1.7
Average		
Mean	7.9 years	
Median	7.5 years	

Other relatives.—Twenty-seven households included one or more relatives,[9] sometimes temporary visitors, sometimes permanent members of the family. Twenty-one of the forty relatives were wholly or partly supported by the family during the time they were in the home. The dependent relatives were usually the grandparents.

Boarders and lodgers.—In comparison with other working-class groups it seems surprising that only two families reported lodgers at the time the study was made, and that the only boarders were three men who roomed elsewhere but took their meals with the family. A procedure more common than taking lodgers was to rent a part of the house as a flat or as light-housekeeping rooms.

Occupations.—The majority of Mexican immigrants in this country are either agricultural laborers, usually migratory, or laborers

[9] Status at time of investigator's visit; nine others reported relatives in the household at some previous time in the year.

engaged in low-skilled industrial occupations. It is not surprising, therefore, to find half the men in this study in occupations classified as "low skilled"[10] and twenty more in semi-skilled work. The former group included twenty-five day laborers, ten cement workers, eight maintenance of way men, and seven men engaged at miscellaneous jobs requiring little or no ability or training. The semi-skilled group included such occupations as gardeners, pantrymen, truck drivers, firemen, janitors. Fifteen were skilled workmen, including a carpenter, a plasterer, a meat cutter, a blacksmith, foremen, cooks, and tailors. In addition to the wage earners there were five men with "white collar" jobs as salesmen, agents, or shop clerks; seven small tradesmen, including a contractor, a tailor, a cobbler, two proprietors of barber shops, and the owners of a fishing boat and of a tortilla factory. One minister represented the professions. Two men were too old or ill to work.

Nearly half the women, forty-four, were gainfully occupied at some time in the year, but their work in most cases was limited to irregular, part-time employment, undertaken to supplement the family income, rather than a customary, full-time job. Of the forty-four women, thirty-two worked in canneries at cleaning and packing fish. Four of them worked full time during part of the year; the others worked broken time. In no case did the canneries provide full-time, year-round jobs. The only woman reporting fifty-two weeks of steady work had an invalid husband and was employed in a laundry. Five women worked as shop clerks, four of them for thirty weeks or more. Two other women worked in laundries; one was a cigar maker and one an office worker for brief periods; one did sewing; one assisted in her husband's store without pay.

Since the great majority of the children were still young, it is natural that but few of them were gainfully employed. Children from the age of eleven onward earned small sums out of school hours. The youngest self-supporting child with a regular, full-time

---

[10] The classification of occupations in the accompanying table can only be suggestive, certainly not final. No satisfactory classification of occupations according to degree of skill is available, and the traditional classification by industry, following the Census, fails to reflect the social and economic status of the worker in his community, which is our chief interest in the present study.

TABLE 6

OCCUPATIONS OF MEN AND WOMEN*

Occupation†	Men	Women
Total..	100	100
None..	2	56‡
I. Professional and executive..........	*1*	....
Minister...................................	1	....
II. "White collar" jobs.....................	*12*	*7*
Small tradesmen.......................	7	....
Salesmen and agents................	3	....
Clerical workers........................	....	1
Shop assistants........................	2	6¶
III. Skilled workmen...........................	*15*	*1*
Foremen......................................	3	....
Cleaners......................................	2	....
Tailors...	2	....
Cooks..	2	....
Others...	6	1
IV. Semi-skilled workers....................	*20*	*36*
Cannery operatives....................	....	32
Kitchen and pantry workers..	4	....
Gardeners...................................	3	....
Taxi and truck drivers............	3	....
Firemen.......................................	2	....
Lumber assorters......................	2	....
Laundry operatives..................	....	3
Others...	6	1
V. Low-skilled workers......................	*50*	....
Day laborers..............................	25	....
Gas company...........................	6	
Street-car company..............	2	....
Cannery....................................	3	....
Odd jobs..................................	4	....
Not specified.........................	3	....
Miscellaneous........................	7	....
Cement workers........................	10	....
Maintenance of way laborers..	8	....
Others...	7	....

* Persons engaged in more than one occupation within the year were classified under that in which they spent the longest time.

† Classification modified from Taussig, *Principles of Economics*, II: 134-137, 1913 ed.

‡ Housewives.

¶ Includes one woman who helped in her husband's shop without pay.

job was seventeen years old. The school children sold papers and junk, ran errands, did odd jobs, or were mothers' helpers. The children of legal working age who were still partly dependent upon their parents, were usually working irregularly in the canneries or laundries, at caddying, or in domestic service. The older, independent ones with full-time work were engaged in much the same occupations as their parents. Four of the six self-supporting girls worked in canneries, one did housework, and one was a waitress. The eight independent boys included a timekeeper and a laborer in the canneries, a mechanic's helper, a cleaner and dyer, a car cleaner, and a laundryman.

III

INCOME

"Income" includes all cash receipts during the year that went into the current family fund, with the exception of money borrowed or drawn from savings. The latter items represent a deficit.[11] Money earned by the children and not contributed to the general family fund[12] was not included, unless the expenses for which it was dis-

TABLE 7
AMOUNT OF TOTAL FAMILY INCOME DURING THE YEAR

Total annual income	Number of families	Percentage of all families
All amounts....................................	100	100.0
Less than $250.00............................	1	1.0
$250.00–$499.99...............................	2	2.0
500.00– 749.99...............................	6	6.0
750.00– 999.99...............................	13	13.0
1000.00–1249.99...............................	22	22.0
1250.00–1499.99...............................	23	23.0
1500.00–1749.99...............................	16	16.0
1750.00–1999.99...............................	8	8.0
2000.00–2249.99...............................	6	6.0
2250.00–2499.99...............................	2	2.0
2500.00–2749.99...............................	1	1.0

Average	
Mean...	$1337.35
Median...	1273.75

bursed, such as clothes, were also reported and included in the budget. Accordingly, "income from children" or "from relatives" applies only to their contributions, not to their total earnings.

[11] In this study the problem of money transferred from one investment to another within the year did not arise.

[12] Nineteen of the thirty-nine working children retained part of their earnings and refused to report how these sums were spent.

In ninety of the 100 families the cash income was supplemented by income in kind from one or more sources, usually home-grown food or culls from the markets, firewood gathered along the beach or tracks, gifts of second-hand clothing, or free medical care. The difficulties of expressing the value of second-hand shoes or clinic care in terms of dollars and cents made it impossible to include such items in the cash total.

Amount of total incomes.—The total annual family income varied from $156.20 in a family where the man had only five weeks' work in the year and the deficit was made up from savings, to $2500 earned by a contracting brick-mason. The average family income was about $100 a month   ($1337.35 per year mean, $1273.75 median). Forty-five per cent of the families reported total incomes between $1000 and $1500, and three-fourths reported between $750 and $1750.

TABLE 8

AMOUNT AND PERCENTAGE OF ANNUAL INCOME FROM SPECIFIED SOURCES

Sources of income	Number of families reporting	Average annual income for families reporting			
		Mean		Median	
		Amount	Percentage	Amount	Percentage
Total income	100	$1337.35	100.0	$1273.75	100.0
Man's earnings	98	1085.41	80.6	1060.25	82.5
Income from other sources	76	360.07	26.7	240.00	18.7
Wife's earnings	43	276.50	20.9	216.00	17.1
Children's contributions	16	502.71	35.2	422.50	29.5
From relatives	22	209.29	15.2	209.00	16.4
In household	15	245.30	18.1	240.00	18.9
Elsewhere	8	115.62	8.1	65.00	4.5
Boarders and lodgers	6	87.02	6.5	55.50	4.4
Property	7*	162.75	10.6	84.00	5.5
Insurance	3	217.67	12.9	49.00	2.8
Pension from Mexico	1	160.00	28.0	180.00	28.0
Other	8	41.69	3.5	40.00	3.3

* Includes one family which sub-let four housekeeping rooms at no net gain.

Sources of income.—About 80 per cent of the average family's income was derived from the man's earnings. The rest of the family income came chiefly from the earnings of wife, children, and relatives living in the household. An occasional family received income from boarders or lodgers, rent from property—a house owned elsewhere, a garage, housekeeping rooms, flats in their own dwelling—gifts of money from relatives outside the household, payments from insurance policies, a pension from Mexico, a repaid loan, or the sale of various possessions, such as a car, a baby buggy, chickens, or jewelry.

TABLE 9

AMOUNT OF MAN'S EARNINGS DURING THE YEAR

Annual earnings	Number of families	Percentage of all families
All amounts...................................	98	100.0
Less than $250.00............................	3	3.1
$250.00–$499.99..............................	6	6.1
500.00– 749.99..............................	9	9.2
750.00– 999.99..............................	24	24.5
1000.00–1249.99..............................	27	27.5
1250.00–1499.99..............................	13	13.3
1500.00–1749.99..............................	10	10.2
1750.00–1999.99..............................	4	4.1
2000.00–2249.99..............................	1	1.0
2250.00–2499.99..............................	....	....
2500.00–2749.99..............................	1	1.0
Average		
Mean..	$1085.41	
Median..	1060.25	

Men's earnings.—The average man in these families earned a trifle over $1000 a year ($1085.41 mean, $1060.25 median).[13] Half the men earned between $750 and $1250. Such low earning capacity was to be expected in view of the occupations in which they were engaged. Considering the general grade of skill, there was less

[13] The Census of Manufacturers, 1929 (Mimeo. release, May 11, 1931) reports the average number of wage earners in San Diego as 3,859, the yearly wage bill as $5,258,177, or average annual earnings of $1363 per wage earner in manufacturing industries.

unemployment than might perhaps have been expected. Fifty-three men worked full-time for fifty weeks or more in the year; seventy-eight were employed for at least three-fourths of the year. In two families the man was an invalid, and the mother or son the chief wage earner.

Women's earnings.—Forty-three women added to the family income of the year.[14] On the whole, these women were working in order to supplement inadequate incomes from other sources, since, with their earnings included, the average income in these families was no larger than in families where the woman did not work. The average yearly earnings of their husbands were $300 lower than in the other fifty-seven families.

The irregular character of the women's employment has already been discussed (page 11). Their average earnings were small, less than $20 a month ($276.50 per year mean, $216 median). Twelve of the forty-three earned less than $100 in the year. Eight, including the five full-time employees who worked more than six months, earned between $500 and $950.

Children's earnings.—Only sixteen families received income from children's earnings; in eight others the children earned small sums for pocket-money or clothes, but contributed nothing to the general family fund. Consequently working children were not an important factor in the income of the group as a whole, income from this source averaging only $80 per year per family for the 100 families. In the families where children were working, however, the average return was high ($502.71 mean, $422.50 median). In two families where more than one child was working, income from this source amounted to $1300 and $1600. The largest single contribution was $950 from one girl of twenty-three, who turned over her entire earnings to her mother. Of the thirty-nine working children, twenty turned over all their earnings and nineteen kept some for spending money, in which case the mother usually did not know the child's total earnings. There appeared to be no difference in the practice of boys and girls in this regard.

---

[14] Another woman worked in the family store, but received no regular wages.

Comparison of the children's earnings with their actual costs of maintenance shows that, of the 358 children, 318, or 88.8 per cent, were totally dependent; 24, 6.7 per cent, earned less than 85 per

TABLE 10

STATUS OF DEPENDENCY OF CHILDREN, CLASSIFIED BY AGE

Status of dependency*	Age of children					
	All ages	Less than 6	6 to 10	11 to 15	16 to 20	21 and over
	Number					
Total..............................	358	135	118	70	29	6
Dependent......................	*342*	*135*	*118*	*70*	*17*	*2*
Totally........................	318	135	118	59	6	......
Partially.....................	24	......	......	11†	11	2
Independent..................	*16*	......	......	......	*12*	*4*
Self-supporting..........	2	......	......	......	2	......
Contributing..............	14	......	......	......	10	4
	Percentage					
Total..............................	100.0	100.0	100.0	100.0	100.0	100.0
Dependent......................	*95.5*	*100.0*	*100.0*	*100.0*	*58.6*	*33.3*
Totally........................	88.8	100.0	100.0	84.3	20.7	....
Partially.....................	6.7	....	....	15.7	37.9	33.3
Independent..................	*4.5*	....	....	....	*41.4*	*66.7*
Self-supporting..........	0.6	....	....	....	6.9	....
Contributing..............	3.9	....	....	....	34.5	66.7

* Children earning less than $12 in the year are classified as *totally dependent;* from $12 to 85 per cent of their maintenance costs, as *partially dependent;* over 85 per cent of their costs, as *independent.* Of the latter, those giving the family more than their own costs were considered *contributing.*

† Of these 11 children earning small sums at part-time employment, 3 were 11 years old, 4 were 13, 1 was 14, 3 were 15.

cent of their own costs; 2, 0.6 per cent, were self-supporting; and 14, or 3.9 per cent, not only supported themselves but also contributed to the support of their parents and brothers and sisters.[15]

---

[15] Children earning less than $12 in the year are classified as *totally dependent;* from $12 to 85 per cent of their maintenance costs, as *partially dependent;* over 85 per cent of their costs, as *independent.* Of the last-mentioned, those giving the family more than their own costs are classed as *contributing.*

No children under seventeen were independent; none under eleven earned anything. Girls were a greater financial liability than boys; of children under fifteen, the boys were more likely to get part-time jobs than were the girls, and once past the legal working age, fewer boys than girls remained totally dependent.

Sixteen is the legal minimum working age in California except in special circumstances. Only eleven, or 3 per cent, of the 323 children under sixteen earned anything. Of the thirty-five childrne sixteen and older, less than half were actually self-supporting. Six of the thirty-five earned nothing and were totally dependent upon their parents. Fourteen were contributing more than their own costs to the family purse.

Contributions of relatives.—In fifteen families a relative was living in the household who paid to the family at least part of the costs of his board and lodging, and often contributed additional sums to the family support. The contributions of such relatives averaged $20 a month ($245.30 per year mean, $240 median), but varied from $22.50 to $779 for the year, the latter sum from two brothers-in-law.

Eight families received money from relatives elsewhere, but in only one case was the money reported to have come from Mexico. In five cases the sum was less than $100 for the year. In no case were large sums sent to cover periods of unemployment or illness, but rather as gifts from more well-to-do relatives.

Other income.—Other sources of income, such as boarders and lodgers, rentals from property, insurance payments, a pension, sale of an automobile or of personal property, were reported by only a few families, and although an occasional family might receive a large sum from one of these sources, such cases were too rare to be of importance to the group as a whole. The average family of the 100 studied received less than 1 per cent of its total income from any of the sources named.

Income in kind.—Only ten families reported receiving no income in kind. The difficulties of evaluation already noted make it impossible to say what proportion of the total income was received in this form, but in many families it is obvious that the cash income was not a completely adequate representation of the goods and services enjoyed during the year. Sixty families reported additions to cash income in the form of food grown in their gardens, milk at reduced rates, slightly wilted and discarded vegetables and fruit from the markets, gifts of food from friends and relatives. Forty-six families received clothing, usually second-hand garments. Forty-seven gathered wood along the tracks or the beach or received it from yards and shops where they worked. The greatest assistance came in times of illness, the nightmare of low-income groups. Almost all these families were eligible for free or part-pay medical care at the hospitals and clinics, and sixty-three availed themselves of this service. Only five of the 100 families paid for hospital care in full, one paid part of the expense, and nineteen received completely free hospital care. Many other miscellaneous gifts were reported by a few families, but none of importance to the group as a whole.

Income per consumption unit.—In comparing the economic status of two Mexican families or of the average Mexican family with families in another study it is not sufficient to base a judgment of relative financial well-being on the size of the income alone. Allowance must be made for differences in size and composition of the family. Other conditions being equal, a couple with $100 a month and one or two young children is obviously better off than a larger family with older children and the same income.

Periodic attempts have been made in cost of living studies to relate income to size of family. The procedure has usually been to translate the household into equivalent adult male units. Thus a comparison of the incomes of two dissimilar families may be made in terms of dollars per adult male. Among the earliest of such scales was the "quet" of Ernst Engel, which was a consumption unit, though not in terms of the adult male. By this scale the expense of an infant at birth was fixed as 100 and ten units were added for each subsequent year until maturity.[16]

---

[16] Engel, Ernst, *Cost of production of human beings* (1883). See Williams, Faith M., "Scales for family measurement," *Proceedings of the American Statistical Association* (March 1930): 135–139.

The most significant attempt at a complete consumption unit scale in this country was made by Sydenstricker and King in an investigation of the budgets of South Carolina cotton mill families in 1917.[17] This was a scale of "ammains" and "fammains," derived from the reports of expenditures of the cotton mill families. The ammain is a unit representing a "gross demand for articles of consumption having a total money value equal to that demanded by the average male in that class at the age when his total requirements for expense of maintenance reach a maximum." The fammain is the unit of a scale of food costs relative to the cost for an adult male. This scale was compiled by adjusting the Atwater scale of caloric requirements by age and sex to fit the actual expenditures of families of specified composition. In computing the scale for articles other than food only those expenditures were included which could be charged directly to one or another member of the family. This latter scale was combined with the food scale, fammains, to arrive at the ammain.

E. L. Kirkpatrick has been actively engaged for the past few years in experiments with an elaborate series of cost consumption units for expenditure studies of farm families.[18] In Kirkpatrick's system each subdivision of expenditure—food, rent, clothing, etc.— has its own scale of relative costs for different ages and sexes, derived from the study in hand. The final scale takes account of the number of persons in the family and the greater possibility of economies in larger families, as well as differences in age and sex. The total expenditure for each item is divided by the number of cost consumption units in the family for that item, and the sum of these quotients gives the total expenditure per cost consumption unit. There is no single index of the number of equivalent adult males in the family as in the "ammain" and similar scales.

[17] Sydenstricker, Edgar, and King, Willford I., "The measurement of the relative economic status of families," *Quarterly Publications of the American Statistical Association*, XVII (1921): 842–857.

[18] See especially "The standard of life in a typical section of diversified farming," Cornell University Agricultural Experiment Station, *Bulletin* 423 (1923); and "Comparison of two scales for measuring the cost or value of family living," *American Journal of Sociology*, XXXVII (1931): 424–434.

Other authors are willing to use a scale of relative food require-ments for different ages and sexes to compute the relative costs for other items and the total family expenditure per equivalent adult male, on the assumption that there is a high correlation between relative food requirements, food costs, and costs for other items according to age and sex.[19]

It seemed inadvisable to adopt any of these scales for use in the present study. Cost consumption units like those of Sydenstricker and King, and Kirkpatrick, which were based on the data gathered from a specific group of families, may be wholly inapplicable to another social group at a later date. The relative cost of children and adults may be greatly changed by differences in standards of living, a higher minimum working age, the increased use of special and more expensive diets for young children, the development of new wants, a change in relative price levels. There is no adequate ground for assuming that the relationship between the costs of a man and a young child which was true for South Carolina mill families in 1917 or for New York farm families in 1922 would hold good for Mexican workingmen's families in California in 1930. The use of a scale designed to measure relative caloric requirements as an indication of relative costs of quite other items appeared indefensible.

In this study, as in others, it was desirable to adopt some method by which families of different sizes could be compared and which would furnish a rough measure of economic well-being regardless of the size of family. No general scale of consumption units was set up which could be applied to all families, because it was felt that 100 families were not an adequate sample on which to base such a scale. Instead, each family was treated separately.

The expenditure per consumption unit in each family was com-puted by combining the food expenditure per equivalent adult male and the per capita expenditures for all other items. The scale of cost consumption units which was used in measuring food expendi-

---

[19] Zimmerman, Carle C., and Black, John D., "How Minnesota farm family incomes are spent," University of Minnesota Agricultural Experiment Station, *Bulletin* 234 (1927). See also Kirkpatrick, "Comparison of two scales."

tures is based on the relative costs of a minimum standard diet for adults and children.[20] The total annual expenditure for food was divided by the number of equivalent adult males fed during the year according to this scale, making allowance for absences. Thus the cost of food per equivalent adult male was obtained.

Expenditures for each of the other categories, such as rent and clothing, were divided by the number of persons in the household whose expenses for this item were paid from general family funds, again making allowance for absences. The sum of the expenditures per capita for items other than food was then added to the expenditure for food per equivalent adult male, giving the total family expenditure per consumption unit. In order to get the number of consumption units per family, the total family expenditure was then divided by the expenditure per consumption unit.[21]

This procedure is not so desirable as a generalized scale suitable to this group would be, because it does not allow for age and sex differences in the cost of items other than food. The available data, however, were inadequate for the computation of such a scale.

---

[20] See below, p. 33.

[21] Example 1.

A household of five persons—man, wife, and three dependent children under sixteen. All members of the household were at home throughout the year.

$ 456.00 total expenditure for food ÷ 4.7 equivalent adult
           male units .... $ 97.02 per E.A.M.
  599.85 all other items ÷ 5 .... 119.97 per capita
          $180.00 housing
            23.05 house operation
            31.80 furnishings
          167.85 clothing
          197.15 other
$1055.85 total family expenditure

    Total expenditure per unit $216.99
       $1055.85 ÷ $216.99 .... 4.9 consumption units

Example 2.

A household of twelve persons—man, wife, nine children, the eldest twenty, the youngest born two months before the close of the year, and the wife of the eldest son, who lived with the family for twenty-two weeks. Other members of the family were at home throughout the year. The eldest son gave the family half his wages, for which he and his wife received food and shelter and the items incidental thereto which appear under "house operation" and "furnishings," and paid their other expenses from his own funds. The second son paid for his own clothes and amusements. These three were charged only

This procedure is more satisfactory than a simple statement of income per capita, because (1) it makes allowance for age and sex differences in the costs of food, the most important single item of the family budget and the item most considerably affected by such differences; (2) it takes account of absences from home for part of the year; (3) it makes allowance for the presence of persons like lodgers, independent relatives, or grown children, who contributed only a part of their income to the general family funds and received only a part of their support, usually board and lodging, from these funds.

The average family in this study consisted of about five consumption units (5.2 mean, 4.9 median), and reported a total expenditure between $250 and $300 per unit per year ($290.18 mean, $265.44 median). Like the total income per family, these sums showed great variation, ranging from $80 per unit per year to $726 per unit.

There appears to be a distinct negative relationship between the number of cost consumption units in the family and the expenditure per consumption unit; in other words, the larger the family the smaller the available expenditure per member. To some extent this may reflect a flaw in the cost consumption scale used, showing that too great weight was given to children relative to adults and that no allowance was made for the possibility of economies in larger families. Since, however, 80 per cent of the average family's income was derived from the father's earnings, and since the men

with their share of the family expenditure for food, housing, house operation, and furnishings—in the case of the girl, for twenty-two weeks only. The youngest child was charged with a share in the family expenses for only ten weeks.

$ 766.50 total expenditure for food ÷ 9.8 equivalent
                adult male units.. $78.21 per E.A.M.
    454.93 ÷ (10+1×10 weeks÷52+1×22 weeks÷52).... 42.88 per capita
            $270.00 housing
            170.48 house operation
             14.45 furnishings
    521.75 all other items÷(8+1×10 weeks÷52)............. 63.71 per capita

$1743.18 total family expenditure

            Total expenditure per unit.............................$184.80
            $1743.18÷$184.80.............9.4 consumption units

were of a class whose maximum earning power comes early in life, there was obviously but little tendency for the total income to increase with the size of the family. Accordingly, the smaller expenditure—that is to say, income—per unit in the large families represents, to some extent, greater poverty.

TABLE 11

TOTAL ANNUAL EXPENDITURE PER CONSUMPTION UNIT

Total annual expenditure per consumption unit	Number of families	Percentage of all families
All amounts	100	....
Not available	7	....
Total reported	93	100.0
$75.00–$124.99	3	3.2
125.00– 174.99	10	10.7
175.00– 224.99	17	18.3
225.00– 274.99	19	20.4
275.00– 324.99	20	21.5
325.00– 374.99	8	8.6
375.00– 424.99	4	4.3
425.00– 474.99	4	4.3
475.00– 524.99	1	1.1
525.00– 571.99	1	1.1
575.00– 624.99	4	4.3
625.00– 674.99	....	......
675.00– 724.99	1	1.1
725.00– 774.99	1	1.1

Average		
Mean	$290.18	
Median	265.44	

Surpluses and deficits.—Forty-three of the 100 families reported that they broke even for the year. Nine had small sums of money— all less than $25—on hand;[22] two refused to say whether they had a surplus or deficit at the close of the year. Forty-six, one of whom refused to tell the amount, reported that expenditures had exceeded

[22] Unlike the usage in certain other studies, money saved or invested during the year is classified among expenditures.

income. These deficits included unpaid bills, usually to the grocery store, money borrowed, and money drawn from savings. Most of the deficits took the form of unpaid bills, which usually amounted to less than $100. Thirty-six families reported unpaid bills, of which all but three were less than $100, and the majority less than $50. Nine families drew on previous years' savings, six of them for sums less than $100. The family that drew out $300 to make the last

TABLE 12

Surpluses and Deficits Reported at Close of Year

Surplus or deficit at close of year	Number reporting	Average amount	
		Mean	Median
Money on hand	9	$ 14.22	$ 15.00
Income and expenditures equal	43	....	....
No report	2	....	....
Deficit	46*	81.75	45.00
Unpaid bills	36†	40.31	30.00
Borrowed	10†	95.00	100.00
Drawn from savings	9	143.89	75.00
Not allocated	2‡	59.00	59.00

* Includes one family which reported a deficit but refused to report the amount; it is therefore not included in the averages.

† Includes one family which reported a $65 deficit covering both bills and borrowings, without indicating the amount of each; the deficit is therefore not included in the averages.

‡ Includes (both in averages and in number reporting) the family mentioned in the preceding footnote.

payment on a house they were purchasing, cannot be considered to have had a true deficit. The family already mentioned, where the man had only five weeks' work in the year, drew out $550 for living expenses. Ten families borrowed money, five less than $100, five between $100 and $200. For the forty-five families reporting deficits the median amount was $45.

Unexplained discrepancies between income and expenditure.—The standard of reliability chosen for the study was that no schedule should be included which showed an unexplained discrepancy between income and expenditure greater than 10 per cent of the income.[23] Without exact household accounts it is, of course, impossible to report with accuracy every expenditure. On the other hand, in an expense estimate the total of which varies greatly from the family's total resources, the accuracy of any of the component detail is doubtful.

In forty-seven families the estimated expenses were less than the reported income after allowance had been made for actual surpluses and deficits; in fifty-three they were more, and in the latter cases the difference tended to be greater. However, of the 100 families, seventy-eight reported discrepancies smaller than 5 per cent of income, and the average was only 3 per cent (3.4 per cent mean, 2.6 per cent median). The average total expenditure exceeded the average total income by $45.33 mean, $75.47 median.

---

[23] One exception was made, a family where income, as defined on page 14, amounted to only $156, supplemented by $550 drawn from savings. The unexplained discrepancy of $32 was 20 per cent of $156, but less than 5 per cent of the total known cash receipts.

IV

EXPENDITURE

Distribution of expenditures.—Food is the chief item in any low-income budget. Among these Mexican families it accounted for more than one-third of the total expenditure[24] (36.6 per cent mean, 35.7 per cent median), or about $500 a year. Housing cost 16 per cent, or slightly over $200; clothing about 13 per cent, or about $175. The costs of house operation—fuel, cleaning supplies, laundry, etc.—amounted to about 5 per cent, or $75. These four major items were a part of the budget of every family, except two families which lived in the section house, rent-free throughout the year. Every family reported expenditures for care of the person, a category which included barber and hairdresser and personal cleaning supplies. This was, however, a small item amounting to 2 per cent of the total, or about $30. All but two families reported expenditures for transportation—carfare and railway fares. Travel expenses greatly increased transportation costs for a few families, but the majority spent less than 25 cents a week, a small fraction of the total expenditure. Automobiles were a disproportionate expense for the twenty-six families which owned them, costing an average of $150 a year. All but one family reported some of the recreational costs grouped as leisure-time activities. The average expenditure for this group of items was about 5 or 6 per cent of the total, or between $75 and $100 a year. Three-fourths or more of the families also reported expenditures for furnishings, insurance and savings, medical care, and charity, the last-named category including gifts to church, to charitable agencies, and to dependents outside the household. Of these, only investments amounted on the average to more than $50 a year. Forty-two families spent small amounts for association dues, and twenty-eight for educational expenses.

---

[24] All such percentages are calculated on the basis of the total expenditure, not the total income, but the two were practically synonymous. (See preceding page.)

Incidental and various miscellaneous expenses in sixty-three families were lumped together in a single category of "other expenses."

For the average family, even in this low-income group, the so-called basic necessaries—food, clothing, the house and its upkeep—took only 70 per cent of the total budget, leaving 30 per cent for

TABLE 13

AMOUNT AND PERCENTAGE OF ANNUAL EXPENDITURE FOR THE MAIN ITEMS OF THE FAMILY BUDGET*

Item	Number reporting	Average annual expenditure for families reporting			
		Mean		Median	
		Amount	Percentage	Amount	Percentage
Total expenditure	100	$1382.68	100.0	$1349.22	100.0
Food	100	506.58	36.6	481.65	35.7
Clothing	100	188.50	13.6	172.71	12.8
Housing	98	225.57	16.2	216.00	15.9
House operation	100	78.74	5.7	69.58	5.2
Furniture and furnishings	89	40.92	3.0	27.90	2.1
Care of the person	100	34.41	2.5	29.60	2.2
Leisure time	99	90.44	6.5	71.00	5.3
Automobile	26	158.68	10.5	142.50	10.1
Other transportation	98	26.31	1.9	12.00	0.9
Investments	80	83.51	5.7	52.20	3.7
Medical care	73	39.06	2.8	30.00	2.3
Associations	42	8.51	0.6	9.00	0.6
Education	28	29.79	1.9	18.00	1.1
Charity	85	16.83	1.2	10.00	0.7
Other	63	61.65	4.3	25.00	1.8

* See also Appendix B.

secondary expenses, of which the most important were leisure-time activities, insurance and savings, and an automobile for those families which owned one.

Food.—The average expenditure for food was about $500 per year per family ($506.58 mean, $481.65 median). Reported expenditures ranged from $242 to $1048, but seldom exceeded $700. Most of this money was spent for food materials to be prepared at home. Thirty-eight families reported costs for meals in restaurants averaging between $30 and $40 a year, usually the husband's or school children's lunches. Thirty reported small miscellaneous food expenses.

Although it was impossible, without a day by day record of purchases, to report exactly the amounts and kinds of food consumed by these families, a general idea of their diet may be obtained from two sources. Eighty-seven families gave detailed estimates of their weekly food expenditure listed by the main categories of foodstuffs—bread, meat, milk, etc. In addition, fifty families reported their daily menus for the week immediately preceding the investigator's visit.

The eighty-seven families which reported details of food expenditures spent an average of $9.50 a week, approximately the average for the whole group. One-seventh was spent for meat, one-eighth for milk, one-tenth for fruit and vegetables, nearly one-half for dry groceries, one thirty-third for butter. Comparing this with the distribution of costs in three standard food allowances for a family of similar composition, it is apparent that the chief dietary errors of the Mexicans consisted in spending too little for milk, butter, fruit, and vegetables, and too much for dry groceries—a category which includes meal for tortillas, frijoles, and other characteristic Mexican dishes. The inadequacy of the butter allowance was especially marked.[25] In comparison with fifty-four laborers' families in Chicago, chiefly Negro and Polish, with slightly higher incomes, the Mexicans showed the same tendency to spend relatively little for butter, fruit, and vegetables, and large sums for dry groceries. The Chicago families, all but two of whose diets were inadequate from a nutritional point of view, spent no greater proportion for milk, and considerably more for meat; in the latter respect the Mexicans' habits more closely approached the standard distributions of food expenditure.

The Mexican immigrant to the United States clings to the diet of his own country.[26] The diet of the working classes of Mexico is

---

[25] Most Mexican families use margarine.
[26] Gamio, *The Mexican immigrant*.

TABLE 14

COMPARATIVE DISTRIBUTION OF AVERAGE WEEKLY FOOD EXPENDITURE IN 87
MEXICAN FAMILIES,* IN THE NESBITT STANDARD FOOD BUDGET FOR A FAMILY
OF COMPOSITION SIMILAR TO THE AVERAGE MEXICAN FAMILY,¶ IN THE OKEY
AND HUNTINGTON STANDARD BUDGET FOR A SIMILAR FAMILY,§ IN THE STAND-
ARD SUGGESTED BY SHERMAN,† AND IN 54 CHICAGO LABORERS' FAMILIES‡

Item	87 Mexican families		Nesbitt standard budget for family similar to Mexican average	Okey and Huntington standard budget for similar family	Sherman suggested standard	54 Chicago laborers' families
	Mean expenditure per family	Percentage of total weekly expenditure	Percentage of total weekly expenditure			
Total per week	$9.50	100	100	100	100	100
Meat, fish, poultry	1.41	15	13	11	}20 or less{	}32
Eggs	.73	8	3	4		
Milk	1.13	12	20	17	20 or more	11
Fruit and vegetables	.94	10	20	26	20 or more	19
Bread, cakes, etc	.66	7	10	12		13
Butter	.30	3	17	9		8***
Dry groceries	4.21	44	17	21	}40**	}17
Candy and ice cream	.10	1	....	....		
Other	.02	....	....	....		

* The other 13 families failed to report details of food expenditure.
¶ Nesbitt, Florence, "Study of a minimum standard of living for dependent families in Los Angeles," *Community Welfare Federation*, Los Angeles, *Bulletin* No. 1 (November 1927).
§ Okey, Ruth, and Huntington, Emily H., "Adequate food at low cost," *Pacific Coast Journal of Nursing*, XXVIII (1932): 279-283.
† Sherman, H. C., *Chemistry of food and nutrition* (1926): 559.
‡ Houghteling, Leila, *The income and standard of living of unskilled laborers in Chicago* (1927), Appendix D.
** Twenty per cent to cereals, part of which are included under "dry groceries," 20 per cent to all other items.
*** Includes other fats.

practically limited to maize and beans, prepared with fats and
sauces in a variety of dishes, coffee to drink, and meat when
finances permit.[27] The menus reported by fifty families confirm the
persistence of native food habits. Of the fifty families, 95 per cent
served tortillas regularly, twice a day in the average family, which

[27] Thompson, Wallace, *The people of Mexico* (1921): 257-286. Redfield,
Robert, *Tepoztlan, a Mexican village* (1930): 39-41.

explains the scarcity of bread and butter shown in table 14. Some women still ground the corn in their own metates, some used commercial meal. The other Mexican staple, beans, was served every day in 72 per cent of the households reporting, and on alternate days in 20 per cent more. Coffee was the chief drink; only ten families reported serving tea at any meal; chocolate was equally rare; milk was seldom served to adults. The average family had meat once a day. Potatoes, rice, and pastes were not popular. In the average family potatoes appeared at about three meals a week, rice and pastes less often than one meal every third day. The most serious deficiency in these diets, as already noted, was a shortage of dairy products, fruit, and vegetables. The menus showed that thirty-eight of the fifty families served no fruit at meals, and five no salad nor vegetables other than potatoes. Only twenty of the fifty families served a vegetable as often as once a day. Equally strange to Americans, but of little dietary importance, is the fact that forty-two of the fifty families never served a dessert of any sort.

The Mexican peon who retained the food habits of his native country would consider himself well fed at the table of the average family studied. It has been asserted that the typical Mexican diet of maize, beans, and fats provides adequate nutritive values in assimilable form for a man engaged in heavy labor, though not for women and children.[28] Obviously, however, it does not provide the milk and butter, fresh fruits and vegetables demanded by accepted modern standards of nutrition, particularly for growing children. The usual argument in such circumstances, that Mexicans are accustomed to poorer food and lower standards of living than North Americans and Europeans, is well answered by Florence Nesbitt:

The greatest care should be used in ascribing to nationality or race any difference in necessary cost of maintaining a minimum normal standard of living. Insofar as this standard is limited to necessities for health there can be no difference based upon these conditions.

A family in one of our recent immigration groups may be content with a standard which does not furnish the minimum necessities, but the effect of

[28] Thompson, *op. cit.*, 280–285.

under-feeding and bad living conditions is just as disastrous to their children as it would be to an American family.[29]

She quotes in proof the infant mortality statistics for Los Angeles (1923) showing the infant death rate of Mexicans to be three times that of the white population.[30] It may be noted in this connection that the outdoor relief budget for the Los Angeles County charities adopted in February 1928, which is also used in San Diego, reduces the standard food budget 20 per cent for Mexican families.[31]

Since no attempt was made to study actual food intake of these families, the adequacy of their diet can be quantitatively measured only in terms of how far their expenditures for food were adequate to meet the cost of a standard ration, which in this instance is the series of diets for persons of different sexes and ages compiled by Florence Nesbitt in Los Angeles in 1927 for the use of the local charities[32] with prices adjusted for the lapse of time. The cost for each person's ration in the Nesbitt budget was computed in terms of the cost for a man at moderate work, or as "equivalent adult male units." Each Mexican household was then translated into terms of these units, making deductions for absences and for meals eaten away from home. The expenditure for food per unit was then computed and compared with the adjusted Nesbitt standard to determine how far each family fell short of the money expenditure necessary to purchase a ration adequate and balanced according to this standard.[33]

---

[29] "Study of a minimum standard of living for dependent families in Los Angeles," *The Community Welfare Federation, Los Angeles, Bulletin No. 1* (November 1927): 34.
  Of course it may be urged that Mexicans get their food more cheaply than was contemplated by this standard diet—as is discussed below—but in view of the general prejudice which tends to drive Mexican allowances far below the level of other national groups, it seems important to preserve the general standard.

[30] In San Diego in 1928 the infant mortality rate was 48 for the city as a whole, 102 for the Mexicans. San Diego County Health Department (letter, December 2, 1931).

[31] San Francisco furnishes a special diet for Mexicans; Alameda County makes no distinction.

[32] *Op. cit.*

[33] Gifts of food and purchases of slightly stale foodstuffs at reduced price will, of course, lower the money expenditure necessary to secure adequate food. See below.

The adjusted Nesbitt allowance for a man at moderate work was $140.92 a year, or 39 cents a day. The average Mexican household in this study—4.5 equivalent adult male units—spent slightly over $100 a year per man ($113.17 mean, $102.78 median), or between

TABLE 15
EXPENDITURE FOR FOOD PER EQUIVALENT ADULT MALE UNIT

Annual expenditure for food per e.a.m. unit		Number of families	Percentage of 93 families
All families..		100	....
Information not available.........................		7	....
Total reported...		93	100.0
Percentage of standard allowance	**Amount spent**		
30.0– 39.9	$42.28–$56.36	3	3.2
40.0– 49.9	56.37– 70.45	8	8.6
50.0– 59.9	70.46– 84.54	10	10.7
60.0– 69.9	84.55– 98.63	17	18.3
70.0– 79.9	98.64–112.73	13	14.0
80.0– 89.9	112.74–126.82	11	11.8
90.0– 99.9	126.83–140.91	9	9.7
– – – – – – – – – – – – – – – standard – – – – – – – – – – – – –			
100.0–109.9	140.92–155.00	9	9.7
110.0–119.9	155.01–169.09	6	6.4
120.0–129.9	169.10–183.19	1	1.1
130.0–139.9	183.20–197.28	4	4.3
140.0–149.9	197.29–211.37	....	....
150.0–159.9	211.38–255.46	2	2.2
Average			
Mean	80.3 per cent	$113.17	
Median	72.9 per cent	102.78	

20 and 25 per cent below standard. The amounts spent per man varied from $50 to $217, or from a 64 per cent deficit to a 53 per cent surplus. Forty-four per cent of the families spent between $85 and $127, that is, from 60 to 90 per cent of the requirement. Eleven families reported deficiencies greater than 50 per cent. The expen-

ditures of sixty-two families were at least 10 per cent below standard, and those of fifty-one families were more than 20 per cent below. Twenty-two families reported spending more than the standard.

The fifty-one families with a serious deficiency in their food expenditures were, on the whole, the larger and poorer families of the group. The average family of the fifty-one whose expenditure for food was 20 per cent or more below standard had one or two more mouths to feed and one-third less total expenditure per consumption unit than the average for the families whose food expenditure was approximately standard or above.

It is obvious that undernourishment, according to accepted dietetic standards, was prevalent in this group of Mexican families, so far as the amount spent for food is an index of the nutritive value of the diet. Certainly two-thirds of the families spent too little to purchase an adequate food supply, and probably their numbers were augmented by others who spent enough to buy the standard allowance, but did not spend it intelligently.

It must be borne in mind that the amount spent for food does not represent all the food consumed in every household. Some families bought slightly wilted fruits and vegetables or stale bread at greatly reduced prices. Others, living on the waterfront, were given fish from the boats. In other cases, deficiencies in food purchased were modified to some extent by the additional food supplies from gardens, chickens, and goats, from vegetables and fruit discarded at the markets or donated by friends and relatives, and from left-overs from restaurants or stores where the man worked. Sixty families reported such additions to their purchased food, but in at least nineteen of these cases the amount was insignificant, worth $15 or less. In most cases it was very difficult to determine the extent of supplementary food, since neither the quantity nor the value was reported. On careful examination of the schedules, it seemed improbable that this extra food ever equalled the amount of the deficit. Of the families which spent less than 80 per cent of the standard allowance, not half received appreciable supplements in food.

Clothing.—The average family spent about $175 a year ($188.50 mean, $172.71 median), or 13 per cent of its total budget, on clothing for its five or six members. Three families of four, five, and eight members respectively, all with annual incomes less than $525, spent less than $50 on clothes for the whole family. The three largest expenditures were between $400 and $500, all in families with incomes of $1800 to $2100.

TABLE 16

NUMBER OF FAMILIES REPORTING A SPECIFIED EXPENDITURE FOR CLOTHING, AND THE NUMBER OF SUCH FAMILIES WHICH RECEIVED GIFTS OF CLOTHING WITHIN THE YEAR

Annual expenditure	Number of families spending specified amount for clothing	Number of families receiving gifts of clothing
All amounts	100	45
Less than $50.00	3	3
$50.00–$99.99	14	7
100.00–149.99	24	13
150.00–199.99	19	9
200.00–249.99	16	3
250.00–299.99	10	4
300.00–349.99	8	3
350.00–399.99	3	1
400.00–449.99	2	1
450.00–499.99	1	1

Average		
Mean	$188.50	
Median	172.71	

About the same amount of the total clothing expenditure, approximately $50, was apportioned to husband and to wife (man: $52.54 mean, $44 median; woman: $51.49 mean, $43.50 median), and about half as much, on the average, to each child in the family (average per child: $25.31 mean, $21.67 median).

The cost of the husband's clothing ranged from $2.90 to $184.50. All but one of the expenditures were less than $120; half were between $25 and $75.

The cost of the wife's clothing covered almost the same range, the highest expenditure being $175.60. Fifty-two per cent of the women spent between $20 and $60; 18 per cent spent less than $20. The average clothing expenditure for employed women was approximately the same as for the housewives. Of the ten women who spent $100 to $175, however, six were employed.

The average expenditure per child for clothing ranged from $1.73 to $69.40 per year. In 60 per cent of the cases the expenditure was between $10 and $30. These figures, like all the expenditures reported in this study, are limited to those items paid from the family purse. Older children who were working and bought their own clothes may have spent more. There was no marked relationship between the number of children in the family and the clothing expenditure per child.

The Mexican immigrant may cling to his native food-habits, but he rapidly adopts American dress. The clothing purchases reported were overalls, wool suits, ready-made dresses, silk stockings, corsets, felt hats, instead of the native muslin trousers and blouse, calico dress, straw hat, and reboso of Mexico. The tables in Appendix A attempt to depict the wardrobe and annual clothing purchases of certain typical persons in the group studied.

The average man bought a $26 suit every four years and a $3.50 hat every two years. He owned no overcoat. His everyday working costume was overalls or separate pants and $1 shirts. He wore neckties only for dress. He did not buy nightclothes. The woman of the family habitually wore cotton house dresses at $1, but she owned two "best" dresses, costing $9 each, two cheap hats, and silk stockings for street wear. A boy of twelve or older, whose clothes were bought by his family, had a new suit every two years. Like his father, his usual costume was a cheap cotton shirt with overalls or pants, cap, and sweater. Girls under twelve wore cotton dresses costing 75 cents apiece, and owned a better dress at $2, which was replaced every second year. Hats, bought every third year, were obviously worn only on special occasions. They wore socks instead of stockings.

Housing costs.—The items included under this category are rent, or interest and installments paid on a house, taxes and assessments, fire insurance, repairs, water, plants and fertilizer for the garden, and garage rent. Families which were renting very seldom paid for any of the other items; water costs were included in the rent seven times out of eight, and only five tenant families reported expenditures for garden or repairs; their housing expenditures may be taken as practically synonymous with rent. Two families lived the whole year, one for ten and one-half months, and one for one month, in the section houses.[34] Eighty-five families (including for certain months the last two mentioned) paid rent; thirteen owned their homes,[35] but nine of these were still paying on the mortgage. No family in this group began to purchase a house in the year of this study.

The owners did not differ appreciably from other families of the group as regards occupation, expenditure per consumption unit, or size of family, but the men were older. None were under thirty, and the average age was thirty-five.

The eighty-four families which rented their living quarters[36] paid on the average about $200 a year ($212.73 mean, $216 median). The most common rentals were $15 and $20 a month;[37] one family spent $30 and another $35. More than half spent between $150 and $250 a year.

---

[34] Maintained by the railroad for trackmen and similar employees. These were one-story buildings with six apartments, one bathroom and one outside toilet, where the railroad workers with families received as part of their wages a two-room, unheated apartment, electricity, and stove wood for cooking.

[35] It is customary in such studies to classify homes mortgaged or being bought on installments as "owned."

[36] Omitting one family which paid rent only for a month and a half, amounting to but $9. This is a much higher proportion of tenancy than was reported by the 1930 census for San Diego as a whole—52 per cent.

[37] The San Diego Realty Board reported $20 a month as the average rental of a workingman's home, $15 to $20 for the Mexican district. The Census of 1930 reported $19 as the median rental for "other races"—of which Mexicans constituted 82 per cent—in San Diego.

TABLE 17

ExPENDITURE FOR HOUSING ACCORDING TO CONDITIONS OF TENURE

Annual expenditure	Number of families spending a specified amount for housing				
	All families	Tenants	Owners		
			All owners	Owned clear	Mortgaged
Number					
Total	100	87	13	4	9
Free housing*	3	3	....	....	....
All amounts	97	84	13	4	9
Less than $50.00	1	....	1	1	....
$50.00–$99.99	2	....	2	2	....
100.00–149.99	15	15	....	....	....
150.00–199.99	24	23	1	....	1
200.00–249.99	28	26	2	1	1
250.00–299.99	10	10	....	....	....
300.00–349.99	8	8	....	....	....
350.00–399.99	3	1	2	....	2
400.00–449.99	3	1	2	....	2
450.00–499.99	1	....	1	....	1
500.00–549.99	....	....	....	....	....
550.00–599.99	....	....	....	....	....
600.00–649.99	....	....	....	....	....
650.00–699.99	1	....	1	....	1
700.00–749.99	1	....	1	....	1
Average†					
Mean	$227.80	$212.73	$325.21	$91.93	$428.89
Median	216.00	216.00	388.00	58.18	404.09
Percentage					
All amounts	100.0	100.0	100.0	100.0	100.0
Less than $50.00	1.0	....	7.7	25.0	....
$50.00–$99.99	2.1	....	15.4	50.0	....
100.00–149.99	15.5	17.8	....	....	....
150.00–199.99	24.8	27.4	7.7	....	11.1
200.00–249.99	28.9	31.0	15.4	25.0	11.1
250.00–299.99	10.3	11.9	....	....	....
300.00–349.99	8.2	9.5	....	....	....
350.00–399.99	3.1	1.2	15.4	....	22.2
400.00–449.99	3.1	1.2	15.4	....	22.2
450.00–499.99	1.0	....	7.7	....	11.1
500.00–549.99	....	....	....	....	....
550.00–599.99	....	....	....	....	....
600.00–649.99	....	....	....	....	....
650.00–699.99	1.0	....	7.7	....	11.1
700.00–749.99	1.0	....	7.7	....	11.1

* Including one family which paid only $9 rent for the year.
† Excluding the family mentioned in the preceding footnote.

Of the thirteen house owners, four carried no mortgage. Their housing costs were naturally low, $65 a year or less for three who paid only very small taxes and assessments, water, and fire insurance. One spent $207, including a heavy assessment, repairs, garden, and a large water bill. The nine who were still paying for their homes had much heavier costs than those who rented, averaging more than $400 a year ($428.89 mean, $404.09 median), and ranging from $196, which included no installments on principal, to $729, of which $500 was installments, paid by that family of the group which had the largest income. All these families also paid taxes and water costs, and seven of the nine paid assessments ranging from $7 to $60. The total taxes and assessments paid by the thirteen owners ranged from $18 to $113, averaging between $50 and $60.

Water costs were usually included in the rent, but eleven tenants in addition to the thirteen owners paid for their own water. The monthly water bills were never less than $1 and usually between $1 and $1.50.

Housing conditions.—Separate cottages were more common than flats.[38] Sixty-one families lived in detached, one-family houses. In this group were found all but one of the owners. Thirty-six were in multiple dwellings, including three which were living in section houses at the time of the investigation and one owner who rented the upper story of his house. Two families lived behind their shops. One failed to report.

Overcrowding was common. The dwellings contained from two to seven rooms, but two-thirds consisted of three or four rooms. For an average household of six persons, the average house had four rooms, or 0.6 rooms per person. Government studies set a standard of one room per person.[39] Seventy-six families, or 80 per cent of those reporting, were below standard, that is, had less than one room per person. The larger the family the more markedly was it

---

[38] According to the Census of 1930, 96 per cent of all dwellings in San Diego were one-family dwellings.

[39] United States Bureau of Labor Statistics, *Minimum quantity budget necessary to maintain a worker's family of five at a level of health and decency* (1920): 13.

TABLE 18

NUMBER OF ROOMS CLASSIFIED BY SIZE OF HOUSEHOLD

Number of rooms occupied	All families	Number of families occupying specified number of rooms — Size of household											
		Two	Three	Four	Five	Six	Seven	Eight	Nine	Ten	Eleven	Twelve	Thirteen
All dwellings	100	1	10	14	17	23	12	15	4	1	...	2	1
Not reported	5	...	...	...	4	...	...	1	...	...	...	...	...
Total reported	95	1	10	14	13	23	12	14	4	1	...	2	1
Two	8	1	2	3	...	1	...	1	...	...	...	...	...
Three	31	...	5	3	8	5	5	2	3	...	...	...	...
Four	33	...	3	4	4	12	4	6	...	...	...	...	...
Five	15	...	...	3	1	4	3	3	...	...	...	...	1
Six	6	...	...	1	...	1	...	2	1	...	...	1	...
Seven	2	...	...	...	...	...	...	...	...	1	...	1	...
Average number of rooms occupied (per household)													
Mean	3.9	2.0	3.1	3.7	3.5	4.0	3.8	4.2	3.8	7.0	......	6.5	5.0
Median	3.8	2.0	3.1	3.8	3.3	4.0	3.8	4.2	3.2	7.0	......	6.5	5.0
Average number of rooms per person													
Mean	0.6	1.0	1.0	0.9	0.7	0.7	0.5	0.5	0.4	0.7	......	0.5	0.4
Median	0.6	1.0	1.0	1.0	0.7	0.7	0.5	0.5	0.4	0.7	......	0.5	0.4

deficient in house room. The worst examples of overcrowding were families of six, eight, and nine persons living in two or three rooms. There was no crowding comparable to tenement conditions; only five families reported as many as three or four persons per room.

The conditions in regard to sleeping arrangements were somewhat better. Forty-three families had at least the equivalent of one single bed per person, and the average for the group was 0.9 beds per person. One household of eight reported beds for only two persons, and one of thirteen, beds for only seven. There were other marked inadequacies. Investigators reported that in most cases pallets on the floor were used instead of beds, since in Mexico the Mexican habitually sleeps rolled up in a blanket on a mat. For this reason it is difficult to judge the adequacy of their sleeping arrangements by American standards.

Sanitary equipment was notably satisfactory. Every house had running water. Seventy-eight per cent of the eighty-eight families which answered this question reported bathrooms. These were private baths in 60 per cent of the cases, and shared, usually with only one other family, in 18 per cent. Nineteen families, or 22 per cent of those reporting, had no bathroom. Families living in separate houses enjoyed markedly better conditions in this respect than families in flats or apartments. Eighty per cent of the former had private baths, and 18 per cent had none; one family shared its bathroom with another family. In multiple dwellings, 23 per cent of the families had a private bath, 27 per cent had none, and 50 per cent shared a bathroom. Only two of the thirteen owned homes had no bathroom. All but two families had water-closets—indoors and private in fifty-two cases. Fourteen private toilets were reported on back-porches or in yards; twenty-eight toilets were shared with neighbors, usually with only one other family. Four families failed to report. In four cases five or six families used the same toilet. These and two privies were apparently the only serious instances of lack of sanitary conveniences. Privies are allowed in San Diego only in such parts of the city as do not have sewer connections.

In addition to adequate sanitary provisions, the majority of houses were supplied with electricity and gas, especially if they were rented flats instead of small owned homes. Ninety were lighted by electricity, ten by oil lamps. Sixty-one were fitted with gas plates or stoves for cooking, frequently with a wood or oil stove in addition. Where gas was lacking, all but three families used a wood stove in preference to oil.

Although the majority of housewives did the family laundry, only eleven had washing machines. The most common labor-saving devices were electric irons and sewing machines, reported by eighty-four and seventy-nine families respectively. Five of the sewing machines were electric. Forty-one families had both an electric iron and a sewing machine.

In one-third of the schedules the investigator made no comment on housing conditions. The other schedules contained comments so heterogeneous that it is impossible to present a general picture of housing conditions other than the facts already cited. The most frequent comments on the type of house were that it was an old dwelling converted into small flats, or a small, lightly constructed cottage. Scarcity of furniture and furnishings was often remarked. Cleanliness and neatness in housekeeping were noted more often than dirt and disorder. About equal numbers of dwellings were reported as sunny and airy or as dark and poorly ventilated. Nine houses were rear cottages. Four dwellings were reported as dilapidated, one as actually condemned, only two as having no yard space.

In summary it may be said that, according to any standard, the majority of families had inadequate space, and that half of them had too few beds. The typical family had a private bath and water-closet, electricity, gas, an electric iron and a sewing machine. To judge from the investigators' comments, not more than a half-dozen of these families lived in actual squalor. Cases in which housing conditions were not up to standard were less serious in the mild climate of San Diego, where much time is spent out-of-doors, than in a more severe climate.

House operation.—The average family spent about $75 ($78.74 mean, $69.58 median) for the costs of running a house, including electricity, gas, and other fuel, ice, telephone, cleaning supplies, laundry, service, and moving. The amounts ranged from $16 to $221, but few families spent over $125, and one-third spent between $20 and $50. The families with very low expenses usually had no gas and electricity or paid for it in the rent, gathered stove wood on

TABLE 19

EXPENDITURE FOR ITEMS OF HOUSE OPERATION

Item	Number of families reporting	Average annual expenditure for families reporting	
		Mean	Median
Total house operation	100	$78.74	$69.58
Fuel and light	98	37.19	31.30
Electricity	73*	15.87	12.00
Gas	53†	24.20	21.00
Wood	16	26.19	30.00
Coal	2	30.50	30.50
Kerosene	41	6.87	4.00
Laundry supplies	100	20.88	17.15
Laundry sent out—regular	39	33.00	26.00
—occasional	20	8.03	6.00
Telephone—regular rate full year	7	30.07	30.00
—other	22	2.56	.98
Service	8	24.00	15.00
Ice	10	9.33	6.00
Moving	20	6.38	5.00
Paint	2	7.15	7.15

* Excludes 7 families which paid costs for only part of year, 8 where costs were included in rent, and 4 which reported gas and electricity together; 8 families had no electricity at any time during the year.

† Excludes 6 families which paid costs for only part of year, 4 which reported gas and electricity together, and 1 which failed to report the cost; 36 had no gas at any time in the year.

the beach and, of course, did their own laundry. The highest expenditures characteristically included regular laundry service and larger light and fuel bills.

Fuel and light.—The largest item in house operation costs was fuel and light ($37.19 mean, $31.30 median) which included gas, electricity, coal, wood, and kerosene. The modal expenditure, one-fourth of all the cases, was between $10 and $20 a year, but seven spent over $75. The highest sum reported was $132. Families living in the section houses received light and fuel free. Those spending less than $10.80 a year—the minimum charge for electricity—either had no electricity and burned kerosene, or it was included in the rent. The minimum charge in San Diego for gas and electricity combined was $19.80 for twelve months; every family paying less than this amount was receiving free either stove wood or light, usually the former. On the other hand, practically none of the families spending more than $50 a year for light and fuel reported any free supplements. It has already been remarked that nearly half the group gathered its wood; Mexican children are trained to pick up driftwood on the beaches. The group average of $3 a month for light and fuel is evidently not the total cash value of the materials actually used. In addition, investigators report that Mexicans are exceedingly careful in not wasting gas and that not infrequently baking is done on a communal basis by groups of families.

Laundry supplies.—On the average, materials for laundry and house cleaning—soap, washing powder, cleansers, polishes, etc.— cost these families about $1.50 a month ($20.88 a year mean, $17.15 median). The estimates ranged from $5 to $79 a year, but half were between $10 and $20, and amounts over $25 were comparatively rare. Families which regularly patronized a commercial laundry spent on the average as much for cleaning supplies as did those which did all their washing at home.

Laundry sent out.—Despite their relatively low incomes and native customs,[40] more than one-third, thirty-nine, of the families reported laundry sent out regularly during at least a part of the year. The average cost was between $2 and $3 a month ($33 a year mean, $26 median). Four families spent more than $52 a year. Most families spending less than $26 a year used the laundries for a limited period or sent out a bundle only once a month.

In addition, twenty families sent out an occasional bundle of laundry, usually when the housewife was ill.

---

[40] There are few commercial laundries in Mexico, even in the larger cities. Thompson, *op. cit.*, 302, 366.

Telephones.—Telephone costs were not an important item in the typical family budget of this group. Seven families had telephones costing $24 to $39 a year; in another, half the cost was charged to a business conducted at home. Four others which paid nothing had the regular use of a telephone, and twenty-one reported tolls for telephone calls ranging from 5 cents to $12, but averaging only $1 or $2 a year.

Service.—People at this economic level do not keep servants. One saleswoman with a full-time job and a young child had a cleaning woman for two hours a month and paid $3 a week to have the child cared for in her absence, a total of $102 for the year. Seven families reported paid help in the house at the time of a confinement, costing from $1 to $22.50. Others relied on the unpaid assistance of relatives and friends during illness.

Ice and other items.—Ice was little used in these families. One household reported buying ice regularly throughout the year; nine others bought for briefer periods. Costs varied from $1 to $3 a month for the period of purchase. No electric refrigerators were reported.

Two purchases of paint for furniture complete the list of items catalogued as "house operation."

Furniture and furnishings.—The investigators frequently commented that the Mexicans' houses were but scantily furnished. Eleven families spent nothing for furniture or furnishings in the year, twenty-six others spent less than $10, and half of those who made purchases spent less than $30 ($40.92 mean, $27.90 median). The smaller sums were usually spent for pots and pans, dishes, brooms, bedding, or other minor items of household equipment. Seven families spent more than $100, the largest sum, $180. In seven cases the expenditures included small amounts for repairs. Forty-one families were buying furniture on installment, the payments averaging $50 a year ($51.72 mean, $49.50 median). The installment payments averaged 3.5 per cent of the total family expenditure; nine families were paying between 5 and 9 per cent. The families reporting installment payments did not differ from the main group in expenditure per consumption unit. Nor did their installment payments reduce their provision for insurance and savings. Certainly the majority of these Mexicans were not burdened by a load of installment payments for furniture.

TABLE 20

EXPENDITURE DURING THE YEAR FOR FURNITURE AND FURNISHINGS

Annual expenditure	Number of families spending a specified amount			
	Total	Installment payments	Other purchases	Repairs
All amounts..................	89	41	86	7
Less than $25.00............	38	9	65	7
Less than $5.00..........	15	....	23	6
$5.00–$9.99.................	11	3	18	1
10.00–14.99.................	4	....	7	....
15.00–19.99.................	6	....	11	....
20.00–24.99.................	2	6	6	....
$25.00–$49.99.................	20	12	14	....
50.00– 74.99.................	11	12	5	....
75.00– 99.99.................	13	5	2	....
100.00–124.99.................	3	2	....	....
125.00–149.99.................	3	....	....	....
150.00–174.99.................	....	1	....	....
175.00–199.99.................	1	....	....	....
Average				
Mean..................	$40.92	$51.72	$17.42	$3.36
Median..........................	27.90	49.50	11.50	3.50

Care of the person.—This category includes the costs of barber and beauty parlor and of personal cleaning supplies. The last-named classification covers the ordinary bathroom-closet drugs and medical supplies, cosmetics, soap, toothbrushes and paste, shaving cream and razor blades, and similar items.

These Mexican families did not economize by cutting the men's and children's hair at home. All but six men patronized a barber, spending most commonly 50 cents or 75 cents a month ($7.53 a year mean, $6 median). One man spent 50 cents a week. In sixty-two families the children's hair was cut by a barber, at an average cost of 60 cents a month. Twenty-three wives reported expenses for haircuts, usually 50 cents a month. Six families reported occasional marcels for some of their members and one family reported other beauty parlor expenses. The average bill for barber and beauty parlor—the latter a rare item—was $14 a year. Five families spent nothing, nine more than $25, none over $50 for the year.

TABLE 21

EXPENDITURE FOR CARE OF THE PERSON'

Item	Number of families reporting	Average annual expenditure for families reporting		Average regardless of number reporting
		Mean	Median	
Total..................................	100	$34.41	$29.60	$34.41
Barber—husband..........	94	7.53	6.00	7.08
—wife....................	23	5.30	6.00	1.22
—children..........	62	7.75	7.20	4.80
Marcels, etc.....................	7	8.79	9.00	.62
Personal cleaning supplies..............................	96	21.56	18.70	20.69

The typical family spent $1.50 to $1.75 a month for personal cleaning supplies ($21.56 a year mean, $18.70 median). The expenditures ranged from $1.25 to $87 for the year, but only six families spent more than $50, and 70 per cent of the families spent less than $25. Four families, all with low total expenditures per consumption unit, spent absolutely nothing for personal cleaning supplies during the year; they used laundry soap for washing and shaving, and did without cosmetics, toothbrushes, and the other small items of this nature, usually considered indispensable.

Total expenditures for care of the person—barber and personal cleaning supplies—averaged about $30 a year ($34.41 mean, $29.60 median), and ranged from $1.25 to $116.55, but exceeded $75 in only three cases.

V

EXPENDITURE (*Concluded*)

Leisure-time activities.—These Mexican families spent more on the various forms of relaxation and recreation grouped under the title of leisure-time activities than on any other category of expenditure, except food, clothing, and housing. Only one family was too poor to spend anything at all for amusements; several amounts were insignificant; expenditures were reported up to $365. The variation in expenditure was great, with no pronounced central tendency ($90.44 mean, $71 median), probably because of the multiplicity of items in the group. Two-thirds of the families spent less than $100. There appears to be a marked relationship between the amount of total expenditure per consumption unit and the amount spent for leisure time activities. As is usual, recreation costs proved elastic, quickly reduced in poverty, and expanded when family finances permitted.

Expenditures in this category do not represent the full recreational resources of these Mexicans. Central agencies, such as the city schools and Neighborhood House, offer entertainments, social contacts, libraries, various amusements, athletics, and in some cases vacations, so that a small money expenditure does not necessarily imply that the family was starved for recreation. The city schools through their evening classes supply many opportunities for amateur entertainments. As far as the Mexicans are concerned, the talent is almost always furnished by themselves; the events are in the nature of "folk" entertainment; therefore the cost to the Mexicans is slight.

The typical Mexican family spent approximately $80 for its recreation and other leisure-time activities. These took a wide variety of forms, but 70 per cent or more of the families patronized the movies, bought tobacco, and provided spending money for their children. More than half the families reported expenditures for commercial amusements other than movies, for newspapers, and for gifts. One-fourth reported purchases of radios, and one-fourth other musical instruments. Expenditures for vacations, social entertainment, reading matter other than newspapers, and hobbies of any sort were comparatively rare.

Eighty-two families reported expenditures for movies, in most cases between $5 and $25 a year ($18.07 mean, $15.30 median).

TABLE 22

EXPENDITURE FOR LEISURE-TIME ACTIVITIES

Item	Number of families reporting	Average annual expenditure for families reporting	
		Mean	Median
Total	99	$90.44	$71.00
Movies	82	18.07	15.30
Other commercial amusements	56	14.17	12.00
Newspapers	52	7.98	6.58
Other reading matter	36	3.15	3.00
Radio—payments	24	48.30	33.80
Other musical instruments and up-keep, including radio upkeep	23	18.59	10.00
Social entertainment	14	14.57	13.48
Vacation	12	39.33	20.00
Spending money—children	71	14.01	10.40
Chewing gum	32	3.09	2.60
Tobacco	75	21.91	19.50
Gifts	56	10.77	8.00
Stationery and stamps	81	3.20	2.00
Other items	28	10.33	5.30

One reported only 40 cents spent during the year; two spent $5 a month. Of the eighteen families which spent nothing for movies, one had free passes and in three other cases the children probably spent their own money for tickets. Of the remaining fourteen, thirteen had less than the average total expenditure per consumption unit. Obviously, as in American families, movie tickets were an essential feature of these Mexican families' spending ways except under pressure of a special need for economy.

Fifty-six families patronized other forms of commercial amusements, including theaters, pool, excursions, and sports events, but none of these was as popular as movies. The average cost of these items was about $12 a year ($14.17 mean, $12 median).

Only one family spent anything for athletics. Such activities are ordinarily provided by schools and other agencies. An alternative for commercial amusements is home recreation, including expenditures for reading matter, musical instruments, especially radios, and social entertainment. There were not more than a half-dozen families in the whole group which lacked not only commercial amusements but also all these other sources of diversion. Fifty-two families bought newspapers, at an average cost of about 50 cents a month; in another the children paid for the paper; in nine other families other reading matter was purchased. Thirty-six families bought books or periodicals; few of them spent more than $3 during the year. Forty-five families spent money on musical instruments and their upkeep. Twenty-four were buying radios,[41] and half of these spent $30 or less for that purpose although one spent $240; two were paying for pianos; six bought phonographs. A cornet, a banjo, a ukelele, three guitars, and three violins were also purchased. Other families spent small sums for sheet music or phonograph records. Fourteen families reported costs of social entertainment, averaging $14, which was for christenings and other fiestas. Other families included the costs of guests in the food bill.

Only twelve families reported expenditures for vacations. In all but one case this consisted of a visit to relatives or friends in California or over the border; the costs were usually below $50.

Hobbies, such as photography or pets, were rare.

In seventy-one families the children received spending money, which usually amounted to less than $25 a year for all the children of the family ($14.01 mean, $10.40 median), and did not usually include the cost of movies. Nor did it include the money retained by working children for their own use. Probably most of it was

---

[41] According to the 1930 census, 51 per cent of all families in San Diego owned or were purchasing a radio.

spent for candy, ice cream, and chewing gum. Purchases of chewing gum out of family funds, averaging $3 a year, were reported by thirty-two families.

Seventy-five families reported expenditures for tobacco; one man received his tobacco as a gift. The average cost per family was $20 ($21.91 mean, $19.50 median). The highest amount was $65.

Expenditures for gifts and for stationery and stamps were also included in this category of expenditure. The latter was a common but minor item, averaging only $2 or $3 a year. Fifty-six families spent money for gifts either to members of the family or to other persons ($10.77 a year mean, $8 median); seventeen spent less than $5; the highest estimate was $35.

Automobile.—Probably only in the United States would one find ownership of an automobile in a group as low in the economic scale as were these Mexicans. One-fourth, twenty-six, of the Mexican families investigated owned and operated an automobile.[42] Nor were these automobile owners drawn exclusively from the families with some surplus over bare necessaries. The average total expenditure per consumption unit was no higher among car owners than in other families. The automobile apparently represents a diversion of money from more essential expenses, especially in view of the comparatively adequate public transportation facilities existing in San Diego. As example, automobile owners seemingly were economizing on food in order to buy gasoline. In only two of the twenty-six families was the expenditure for food per equivalent adult male equal to the standard; and twenty-one families, or 81 per cent, showed serious deficiencies in contrast to 45 per cent of the families which did not own cars.

Ownership of an automobile was in no sense an economy; the average automobile-owning family saved no more than $3 to $10 a year in carfare compared to families without automobiles. The

---

[42] In addition, one family owned an automobile which was not in use during the year, another a car for business purposes, a third had the use of the employer's car, and in a fourth family all the operating expenses were paid by a grown son. None of these families paid any automobile expenses during the year. Therefore, they are excluded from the group of automobile owners in the following consideration of expenses.

typical automobile among these Mexicans had been bought at second-hand for a comparatively small sum, was three to five years old at the time of this study, and cost about $10 a month for upkeep. Nine families either bought a car within the year or made payments on one previously bought. The sums paid ranged from $35 to two payments of approximately $200 each. All cars purchased in the year in which this study was made were second-hand.

TABLE 23

EXPENDITURE FOR AUTOMOBILES

Annual expenditure	Number of families spending a specified amount		
	All automobile costs	Payments on purchase price	Upkeep—cars owned during full year
All amounts..................	26	9	19*
Less than $50.00...........	3	2	....
$50.00–$99.99...............	7	5	8
100.00–149.99...............	5	....	5
150.00–199.99...............	3	1	2
200.00–249.99...............	3	1	3
250.00–299.99...............	2	....	1
300.00–349.99...............	....	....	....
350.00–399.99...............	3	....	....
Average			
Mean..........................	$158.68	$93.78	$135.81
Median.........................	142.50	76.00	128.00

* Excludes 5 cars operated less than a full year, one case where the employer paid for gas and oil, and one which covered the expenses on 2 cars.

In fact, only two of the twenty-six cars were bought new. Excluding seven cases where the cost of upkeep was for less than a year, was partly paid by an employer, or covered more than one car, the cost of upkeep for a full year ranged from $64.50 to $267—the mean, $135.81, the median, $128.

Other transportation.—Every family but two, both of which had the use of an automobile, spent something for carfare. In addition, two received free street-car passes worth $1 a week. The average

TABLE 24
EXPENDITURE FOR TRANSPORTATION

Annual expenditure	Number of families spending a specified amount			
	Total transportation costs*	Carfare		Travel costs other than vacations
		Automobile owners	Others	
All amounts	98	24†	71‡	13
Less than $25.00	64	21	47	9
Less than $5.00	*13*	*4*	*10*	....
$5.00–$9.99	*18*	*6*	*11*	*2*
10.00–14.99	*21*	*9*	*16*	*4*
15.00–19.99	*9*	*1*	*9*	*2*
20.00–24.99	*3*	*1*	*1*	*1*
$25.00–$49.99	17	2	11	*2*
50.00– 74.99	13	1	11	....
75.00– 99.99	....	....	....	....
100.00–124.99	2	....	1	*1*
125.00–149.99	....	....	....	....
150.00–174.99	1	....	1	....
250.00–274.99	....	....	....	1
275.00–299.99	....	....	....	....
300.00–324.99	1	....	....	....

	Average			
Mean	$26.31	$13.50	$23.55	$41.62
Median	12.00	10.20	12.80	15.00

* Includes $18.60 spent by one family for a bicycle.

† Excludes one family with a free street-car pass. One automobile-owning family spent nothing for carfare.

‡ Excludes one family with a free street-car pass and one with the use of a car.

cost of carfare for families owning automobiles was about $1 a month ($13.50 mean, $10.20 median).[43] Families which depended wholly on street-cars for transportation showed a much greater variance in expenditures, depending on whether the man and children walked or rode to work or school ($23.55 mean, $12.80

[43] The two families with passes and one with the use of a company car are excluded from this comparison.

median). Some of these expenditures were less than $1 for the whole year, thirteen over $50, and two over $100. Distances are not so great in San Diego as to prevent walking to and from the places of work.

Travel expenses in connection with a vacation have already been discussed under that heading. Thirteen families spent various sums —all but two less than $50—for trips to surrounding towns in search of work, or in one case back to Mexico for a funeral.

One family bought a bicycle for $15 and spent $3.60 for repairs.

Investments.—This category includes investments proper, that is, purchases of income property, life, health, and accident insurance premiums, and bank savings. It does not include installments paid on a house in which the family is living, for such a house is a durable use-good rather than a long-term investment and has therefore been classified under "housing." No attempt was made to ascertain the family's total holdings in the form of bank savings or income property, because of the antagonism such questions would arouse. The amount laid by during the current year has been used as sufficiently indicative of the financial status, since it is improbable that any of these families owned sufficient property to render current savings unnecessary.

Of the 100 families, eighty reported an expenditure for some form of investment, but in three cases it was merely small sums put aside in the children's school savings. The amounts reported ranged from $5 to $427 for the year. The average was less than $100 ($83.51 mean, $52.20 median). Two-thirds reported less than $75.

Obviously, therefore, about one family in four of these Mexicans could make no provision during the year for sickness, old age, or death; and certainly many, if not most, of the other families were making no adequate provision against serious illness or death of the breadwinner.

Life insurance was the most usual form of investment, carried by some person in every one of the seventy-seven families that reported any type of investment other than children's school savings. The average annual premiums paid per family were about $40 ($41.74 mean, $39 median). Usually the premiums amounted to less than $75 a year; seven families spent more. In the average family this amount covered life insurance premiums for four persons. Attempts to ascertain the face value of the policies proved futile,

TABLE 25

EXPENDITURE FOR INVESTMENTS DURING THE YEAR

Annual expenditure	Number of families spending a specified amount				
	All investments	Insurance premiums	Savings		Other
			Family	Children	
All amounts..............	80*	77	25	16	3
Less than $25.00......	17	22	4	12	....
$25.00–$49.99..........	21	28	1	4	....
50.00– 74.99..........	14	20	3	....	....
75.00– 99.99..........	4	3	1	....	....
100.00–124.99..........	8	3	9	....	1
125.00–149.99..........	2	1	1	....	1
150.00–174.99..........	4	....	2	....	....
175.00–199.99..........	2	....	1	....	....
200.00–224.99..........	2	....	....	....	....
225.00–249.99..........	....	....	2	....	1
250.00–274.99..........	1	....	1	....	....
275.00–299.99..........	3	....	....	....	....
300.00–324.99..........	1	....	....	....	....
425.00–449.99..........	1	....	....	....	....
Average					
Mean..........................	$83.51	$41.74	$109.06	$14.74	$168.33
Median......................	52.20	39.00	120.00	11.88	145.00

* Three of these families reported small amounts for children's savings and no other form of investment.

since most of the Mexicans were either ignorant or misinformed about the policy for which they were paying. The size of the premiums per person, however, makes it obvious that only burial insurance was carried in most cases. Those who carried no insurance were not, on the whole, protected by membership in mutual benefit associations. Only six of the twenty-five with no commercial insurance belonged to a lodge or a union and only one paid dues large enough to cover insurance premiums.

Twenty-five families reported bank savings for the year in addition to insurance premiums; the largest, $250; the most common estimate, $120 ($109.06 mean, $120 median). None of the families which made savings reported insurance premiums of more than $65. All but one of the families reporting bank savings had a total expenditure per consumption unit well above the average for the 100 families.

Two families bought lots within the year, and one invested $145 in stocks and bonds.

In an attempt to ascertain the circumstances which enabled these Mexicans to provide for the future, a comparison has been made between the twenty-three families with no investment or savings of any type within the year, or with only children's school savings, and the twenty-four families which reported amounts in excess of $100.[44]

The most striking differences between the two groups of families were that those which saved over $100 during the year had an average total expenditure per consumption unit twice as great as that of those families which saved nothing, and that, in the former group, twice as many heads of families were steadily employed throughout the year. In other words, the reports of appreciable savings came from those families which were most comfortably situated, with incomes comparatively steady and large in proportion to the number of persons in the family.

Such being the case, these families were able to save without unduly curtailing either necessaries or luxuries in their budget. The families which saved over $100 spent three times as much on leisure-time activities as those which saved nothing, and as high a proportion owned automobiles. Their expenditure per consumption unit for food was larger and the proportion of serious deficiencies smaller.

---

[44] That is, a total for the year of $100 for the category "investments," including life and accident insurance premiums, bank savings, stocks, real estate.

Because any serious illness among these Mexicans was cared for free or at greatly reduced rates, the costs of sickness do not appear as a major impediment to savings, as is often true in other groups. In this respect there was no appreciable difference between those with large savings and those with none.

The future of the twenty-three families without insurance or savings was not provided for by other forms of investment. Only one of the group owned or was buying a house, and only one paid mutual benefit dues large enough to provide insurance.

In brief, the Mexican families which made provision for the future were those with an available surplus after other needs had been supplied. One-fourth of the whole group carried no insurance and made no savings in this year. In the majority of cases there was little or no provision made beyond funeral costs.

Medical care.—It has become axiomatic that the poorest and the richest classes receive the best medical attention. As has already been mentioned, most of these Mexican families were eligible for free or part-pay medical care, and sixty-three reported receiving such care at some time in the year. Accordingly, sickness did not constitute such a drain on the budget as in working-class families of a higher income level, and there were few cases where a serious illness financially crippled the family.

Twenty-seven families reported no costs for medical care. Of these, seventeen received no attention whatever within the year and ten were cared for free of charge. Fifty-three others paid a part of their own costs, and twenty were entirely self-sustaining. In the latter families, which paid all their own costs of medical care, the amounts reported ranged from $3 to $82, the average less than $30 ($31.76 mean, $26.25 median). The average expenditure in the fifty-three families which received free or part-pay care was slightly higher ($41.81 mean, $30 median).

Taken together, seventy-three families which paid for part or all of their medical care spent an average of less than $40 a year ($39.06 mean, $30 median). The largest sum reported was $123. Of the ten families which spent more than $75, only one was unassisted by free or reduced-cost care. The only evidence of severe hardship arising from the cost of illness was in three families whose bills for medical care exceeded 10 per cent of the total family expenditure.

In the schedule the costs of confinement were not separated from other medical expenses, but judging by the total bill for medical

TABLE 26

EXPENDITURE FOR MEDICAL CARE

Annual expenditure	Number of families spending a specified amount							
	All medical costs			Doctor	Dentist	Drugs	Hos-pital	Other
	All families	Paid in full	Paid part only*					
All amounts................	73	20	53	56	21	47	6	17
Less than $10.00........	8	2	6	9	10	28	....	9
$10.00–$19.99.............	17	5	12	13	7	16	....	5
20.00– 29.99.............	11	4	7	14	1	1	....	2
30.00– 39.99.............	9	2	7	8	2	1	1	1
40.00– 49.99.............	7	3	4	5	....	....	....	....
50.00– 59.99.............	4	2	2	2	1	....	2	....
60.00– 69.99.............	2	....	2	3	....	....	....	....
70.00– 79.99.............	6	1	5	....	....	....	2	....
80.00– 89.99.............	3	1	2	....	....	....	1	....
90.00– 99.99.............	2	....	2	....	....	1	....	....
100.00–109.99.............	....	....	....	1	....	....	....	....
110.00–119.99.............	1	....	1	1	....	....	....	....
120.00–129.99.............	3	....	3	....	....	....	....	....
Average								
Mean............................	$39.06	$31.76	$41.81	$27.67	$12.90	$10.23	$60.83	$10.87
Median.........................	30.00	26.25	30.00	25.00	10.00	8.00	62.50	8.80

* This includes the total expenditure for medical care of all families which received any care at clinic rates. Some such families, of course, paid in full for all but one item, such as dentistry. The sum of this column is therefore greater than the total expenditure for clinical care, $938.55.

care in twenty-four families where a child was born within the year, the costs of childbirth averaged less than $50 and rarely exceeded $100. The most usual doctor's fee in such cases was $25. Eight, or one-third, of the confinements were in a hospital, three receiving free care and one reduced rates. Ten families paid the full costs of childbirth.

Of the $2851 spent for medical care during the year in this group of 100 families, $1549, 54 per cent, was spent for doctors; $481, 17 per cent, for drugs; $365, 13 per cent, for hospitals; $271, 10 per cent, for dentists; and the remainder, $185, 6 per cent, for miscellaneous items. Of the total amount, 33 per cent was only part-payment for the services received, and about half the families received completely free care in addition.

About half the families paid a small doctor's bill and bought some drugs within the year. One family in five paid a dentist's bill, and only six of the 100 paid anything for hospital care. Forty-three per cent of the dentists' bills, 34 per cent of the bills for doctors, 35 per cent of the miscellaneous bills, 28 per cent of the payments for drugs, and one of the six hospital bills, were only part-payment for the care received. Completely free hospital care, reported by nineteen families, was more common than part-pay; little free dental work was reported. It seems safe to assume that three-fourths of the Mexican children received no dental care within the year.

The average bill for the doctor was $25; for the dentist, $10; for drugs and for miscellaneous items such as eye-glasses, x-rays, and laboratory tests, less than $10. As has been already mentioned, the average total bill for medical care was less than $40 a year in those seventy-three families which paid anything for this item.

Associations.—Group activities, at least of societies which collected dues, played little part in the lives of these Mexicans. Less than half the families, forty-two, paid dues in any sort of association. Their situation differed sharply from that of Mexican immigrants in earlier studies and low-skilled labor in general. The *mutualistas,* societies combining mutual benefits for sickness and burial with social functions, and the variety of other social organizations noted by observers elsewhere,[45] were scarcely represented. Among the 100 families only four reported such memberships, two in the Unión Patriótica Benéfica Mexicana Independiente, one in

---

[45] Gamio, *Mexican immigration,* 131–136.

Taylor, Paul S., *Mexican labor in the United States* (University of California Press, 1930–1931), I: 62–64, 184–185, 359–360; II: 131–142.

the Alianza Hispano-Americana, and one in the Woodmen of the
World. One belonged to a motorists' association, and six to purely
social organizations with nominal dues.

On the other hand, thirty-two men belonged to some sort of union
or employees' association, often with benefits attached, although
the dues rarely exceeded 75 cents a month. This proportion is high
for any group so predominantly low skilled or semi-skilled as this
one. It is almost incredible for Mexicans, who, because of non-
citizenship, are habitually excluded from unions associated with
the American Federation of Labor. Some of these so-called union

TABLE 27

EXPENDITURE FOR ASSOCIATION DUES

Item	Number reporting	Average annual expenditure for families reporting	
		Mean	Median
All associations	42	$ 8.51	$ 9.00
Unions	32	7.84	9.00
Lodges, etc.—with insurance	4	17.58	18.30
Motorists' association	1	12.00	12.00
Social clubs, etc.	6	4.00	3.00

dues were paid to employees' associations with benefit features, as
in the case of the six laborers working for the gas company and
two working for the street car company. On the other hand, skilled
trades unions were represented. The two cooks and the two barbers
were union men, and two-thirds of the tailors and taxi or truck
drivers. Five of the ten cement workers were union members, and
three of the four fishermen and fish salesmen. The other seven
union men were engaged in skilled or semi-skilled occupations.

None of the women, most of whom were employed irregularly in
the canneries, reported union affiliations.

Education.—In eighty-two families there were children of school
age, that is, six to sixteen. None of these children attended parochial
or other private schools charging tuition, but some of them had
small expenses for supplies in the public schools and some were

taking music or dancing lessons. An occasional family reported costs for summer school, night school, or day nursery. Twenty-eight families reported at least one of these educational costs. Of the amounts spent, 36 per cent were less than $5; the highest was $122 ($29.79 mean, $18 median). Sixteen families, one in five of those

TABLE 28

EXPENDITURE FOR EDUCATIONAL ITEMS

Annual expenditure	Number of families spending a specified amount						
	All items	Public school expenses	Music or dancing lessons	Summer school	Night school	Day nursery	Parents' education
All amounts...............	28	16	13	3	2	3	2
Less than $25.00...............	16	16	7	3	2	....	2
Less than $5.00...............	10	10	....	....	2	....	2
$5.00–$9.99...............	1	2	....	....	....	....	....
10.00–14.99...............	....	4	1	....	....	....	....
15.00–19.99...............	5	....	6	2	....	....	....
20.00–24.99...............	....	....	....	1	....	....	....
$25.00–$49.99...............	6	....	2	....	....	2	....
50.00– 74.99...............	1	....	....	....	....	....	....
75.00– 99.99...............	3	....	3	....	....	1	....
100.00–124.99...............	2	....	1	....	....	....	....
Average							
Mean...............	$29.79	$4.98	$42.92	$17.50	$4.10	$45.00	$.30
Median...............	18.00	3.95	18.00	17.50	4.10	30.00	.30

with school children, reported minor expenses at public schools, for supplies, books, dues, etc. Such expenses averaged $4 to $5 per family and never exceeded $14. Thirteen families provided music or dancing lessons for their children at costs ranging from $10 to $120 a year ($42.92 mean, $18 median). Three families sent a child to summer school, of which the costs were $15 to $20. Two paid $3.70 and $4.50 respectively for grown sons at night school. Three wives, two of them gainfully employed, left young children at day nurseries for part of the year at an expenditure of $25, $30, and $80. Two families reported expenditures of less than $1 during the year for supplies in classes attended by the parents.

Charity.—All but fifteen of these Mexican families made contributions to dependent relatives, charitable causes, or the church.

TABLE 29

EXPENDITURE FOR CHARITY

Annual expenditure	Number of families spending a specified amount				
	Total charity	Dependents	Church	Charitable agencies	Other
All amounts..............	85	33	62	50	1
Less than $5.00........	32	1	30	47	....
$5.00–$9.99..............	10	1	14	3	....
10.00–14.99..............	9	4	15	....	....
15.00–19.99..............	9	9	2	....	....
20.00–24.99..............	7	5	1	....	....
25.00–29.99..............	6	5	....	....	....
30.00–34.99..............	3	3	....	....	....
35.00–39.99..............	3	....	....	....	....
40.00–44.99..............	3	2	....	....	....
45.00–49.99..............	....	....	....	....	1*
50.00–54.99..............	....	....	....	....	....
55.00–59.99..............	....	....	....	....	....
60.00–64.99..............	....	1	....	....	....
110.00–114.99............	1	....	....	....	....
115.00–119.99............	....	....	....	....	....
120.00–124.99............	....	1	....	....	....
125.00–129.99............	1	....	....	....	....
155.00–159.99............	....	1	....	....	....
160.00–164.99............	1	....	....	....	....
Average					
Mean..........................	$16.83	$28.15	$6.06	$1.62	....
Median......................	10.00	20.00	5.00	1.00	....

* Gift to a sick friend.

The thirty-three families which contributed to dependents included three which sent regular allowances of $5 or $10 a month to a mother in Mexico. The others sent occasional sums, all less than $50 a year, to brothers, sisters, aunts, or more usually to parents. In almost every case these relatives were in Mexico. The average amount given to dependents was not large ($28.15 mean, $20 median) and the families which contributed were drawn, on the whole, from those with a total expenditure per consumption unit above the average.

Fifty families contributed to organized charity in small amounts, usually $1 or $2, never over $5 ($1.62 mean, $1 median). The average total expenditure per consumption unit was slightly higher in these families than in the group as a whole. One family gave $45 to a sick friend.

The contributions to church of sixty-two families ranged from 25 cents to $24, averaging $5 or $6 a year. The families which contributed apparently did so regardless of the amount of their incomes.

There was no tendency to consider one of these forms of charity as a substitute for the other. Families which gave to organized charity were as likely to contribute to the church and to the support of dependents as were those which did not.

Other expenses.—Sixty-three families reported items not included in the above categories. Thirty-six reported lump sums for unitemized "incidentals," ranging from $6 to $30 and averaging $16. Twenty-four repaid debts contracted in previous years. Three of these amounts exceeded $100; half were less than $50. Ten loaned money to others, eight reporting sums of $50 or less, and one of $250. Six paid for funerals that cost between $10 and $175. In five families the man was working away from home for part of the year and had to pay board and lodging in amounts between $30 and $240. Five other families reported miscellaneous small expenses.

TABLE 30

Expenditure for Specified Residual Items

Annual expenditure	Number of families spending a specified amount					
	Inci-dentals	Debts repaid	Loans to others	Funerals	Board and lodging —man	Other expenses
All amounts....................	36	24	10	6	5	5
Less than $25.00..........	33	3	4	1	....	4
Less than $5.00........	....	....	....	....	....	1
$5.00–$9.99.................	1	....	1	....	....	....
10.00–14.99.................	12	2	2	1	....	1
15.00–19.99.................	6	....	1	....	....	2
20.00–24.99.................	14	1	....	....	....	....
$25.00–$49.99..............	3	9	3	3	3	1
50.00– 74.99.................	....	4	1	....	....	....
75.00– 99.99.................	....	5	....	....	....	....
100.00–124.99.................	....	....	1	....	....	....
125.00–149.99.................	....	....	....	1	....	....
150.00–174.99.................	....	....	....	....	....	....
175.00–199.99.................	....	1	....	1	....	....
200.00–224.99.................	....	1	....	....	1	....
225.00–249.99.................	....	....	....	....	1	....
250.00–274.99.................	....	....	1	....	....	....
275.00–299.99.................	....	....	....	....	....	....
300.00–324.99.................	....	1	....	....	....	....
Average						
Mean.............................	$16.28	$68.77	$58.10	$70.00	$111.70	$17.57
Median............................	16.50	45.00	35.00	37.50	48.00	15.00

VI

SUMMARY

The typical Mexican family.—The typical family in the group of Mexicans studied consisted of father, mother, and three or four children under sixteen, the parents born in Mexico, the children in California. The man was usually engaged in low-skilled or semi-skilled work, earning about $1000 a year. In a trifle less than half the cases the woman was gainfully employed, usually in a cannery, for part of the year. The children, on the whole, were still dependent. The average family had income to supplement the man's earnings from some source, such as wife's or children's earnings, or contributions from relatives, which raised its total money income to about $1300 a year. In addition, the average family received income in kind—food, second-hand clothing, firewood, free or part-pay medical care. Approximately half the families broke even at the end of the year, half ran slightly behind.

The costs of food amounted to one-third of the average family expenditure, about $500 a year, but this was insufficient to provide a minimum standard diet. On the whole, these people still clung to their native Mexican food habits—beans and tortillas, few vegetables or dairy products. American clothes, on the contrary, had entirely replaced Mexican dress. The average family spent about $50 each for the husband's and wife's clothing each year and about $25 for each child. The total clothing expenditure amounted to 13 per cent. The average family was much better housed than would have been possible in Mexico, although overcrowding prevailed. For $20 a month it rented a three- or four-room house with bathroom and toilet, electricity, and gas. The majority of families did not have a washing machine, a telephone, household service even in times of illness, ice, or commercial laundry service, although laundry bills were reported in a surprisingly large number of families, marking the progress of Americanization. Less than half the families were buying furniture on the installment plan and the payments were not unduly heavy. Men and children had their hair cut by the barber.

The typical family found its chief recreation in the movies, with occasional patronage of some other form of commercial amusement, bought a newspaper, gave the children about $1 a month for candy and ice cream, spent $20 a year for the man's tobacco. Between 5 and 6 per cent of the average family budget was devoted to leisure-time activities. One family in four was buying a radio. One family in four owned a second-hand automobile which cost $10 a month to operate. The others spent $1 to $2 a month for carfare. The average family apparently had little set aside for illness or the death of the breadwinner. It carried burial insurance policies on four persons, with total annual premiums of $40. One-fourth of the families saved about $10 a month during the year; one-fourth made no provision of any sort for the future. The costs of illness were not a heavy burden, since the average family received part of its medical care free or at reduced rates, and thus spent only $40 a year. Most of this went to doctors. Dentistry was obviously neglected.

One-third of the men belonged to unions or employees' associations, very few to mutual benefit societies or purely social organizations. Expenses for school or lessons were rare. The average family contributed small amounts to church and to charity. One-third of the families sent small money gifts to relatives in Mexico. One-fourth were repaying debts contracted in previous years.

On the whole these Mexican families, typically immigrants though they were, had adopted the American standard of living to a large extent, with the notable exception of their diet. The chief examples of this tendency were the clothing worn, the good housing conditions, and the fact that 30 per cent of the average budget went for items other than the "necessaries" of food, clothing, and shelter.

VII

COMPARISON WITH OTHER COST OF LIVING STUDIES

The preceding sections have outlined the way of living of an immigrant working-class group, in so far as it is represented by the expenditures of a year. The following pages show the similarities and differences between the Mexicans' habits of expenditure and those of a number of other working-class groups in this country and of one group of federal employees in Mexico.

Six working-class groups have been selected: two studied twenty-five years ago—New York tenement dwellers and Pennsylvania steel workers; those in a country-wide study of wage earners in 1918–19; and those in three recent studies of unskilled and semi-skilled workers in Oakland, California, in Chicago, and in the Ford plant at Detroit. In all but one of these groups the income was higher than that of the average Mexican family in the present study, allowing for changes in price levels, and the family was smaller in every case, putting the Mexicans at an additional economic disadvantage. The study of Treasury employees in Mexico was chosen as being the only adequate cost of living investigation in that country in recent years, although for our purpose a study of a group of wage earners would have been more satisfactory.

Comparison with the older studies shows the growth of secondary wants, such as automobiles, radios, and movies, that has taken place in the last twenty years. The emphasis of Mexican spending is for these new wants at the expense of food, housing, and savings. The other recent studies show the same trend, but tend, with larger incomes, to provide more fully for the necessaries of life before money is spent for amusements. A larger percentage of Mexicans reported substandard food expenditures than is found in any other study, except perhaps in that of 1918–19 where it was impossible to make a direct comparison. More overcrowding is found among the Mexicans than in any other group except the New York City residents. On the other hand, the growing public control of sanitation and the spread of modern housing conveniences in California have made the Mexicans better off in these respects than families in earlier studies. The Mexican families appear to be less thrifty. They reported less insurance or savings and fewer affiliations with organizations that offer benefit features. The proximity to Mexico and the possibility of a return there in case of want may afford a partial explanation.

New York City, 1907—workingmen.[46]—Twenty-five years ago Robert Chapin made a study of the "essentials and cost of a normal standard of living" for the New York State Conference of Charities and Corrections, for which 391 expenditure records were gathered from workingmen's families in New York City. The families included were limited to those with not less than two or more than four children under sixteen, and preferably with incomes from $500 to $1000.[47] The sample was predominantly of European immigrants, who constituted 70 per cent of those studied, but it did not represent any single national group. Because of the qualifications set up for inclusion in the study, the average family of 5 persons, was slightly smaller than the average Mexican family of 5.6 persons. As always in large cities, lodgers were more common in the New York study, reported by 34 per cent of the families, as contrasted with 2 per cent of the Mexican families in the present study.

A combination of the cost of living index in Douglas' *Real Wages in the United States, 1890-1926* and the current index of the United States Bureau of Labor Statistics shows that the general price level for the country as a whole in terms of the consumer's dollar was some 75 per cent higher in 1929–30 than in 1907. On this basis, and making no allowance for price differences due to locality, the purchasing power of an income of $800 in 1907, the average for the New York families, was about $1400 in 1929–30. The average Mexican family's income was about $1300.

---

[46] Chapin, Robert C., *The standard of living among workingmen's families in New York City*, Russell Sage Foundation (1909).

[47] Following Chapin's example we quote figures for only 318 families which had incomes between $600 and $1100.

The man's earnings constituted a higher proportion of the family income, 89 per cent, in the New York families than among the Mexicans, 80 per cent. Eighteen per cent of the New York women were gainfully employed within the year in contrast to 43 per cent of the Mexican women. Apparently families with children over sixteen were excluded from the New York study, so that children's earnings were a minor factor in the family income.

TABLE 31

PERCENTAGE DISTRIBUTION OF EXPENDITURES BY NEW YORK WORKINGMEN'S FAMILIES—CHAPIN, 1907—COMPARED WITH MEXICANS

Items	Percentage of total expenditure excluding savings*	
	New York workingmen	San Diego Mexicans
Total expenditure..............................	100.0	100.0
Food...	44.8	37.6
Clothing...	14.0	14.0
Housing..	20.8	16.4
Fuel and light.................................	5.1	2.7
Insurance...	2.4†	2.4
Medical care....................................	2.2	2.1
Carfare...	1.7	1.5
Other..	9.0	23.3

* Regardless of the number of families reporting each item.
† Includes property insurance, excludes insurance carried by mutual benefit associations.

Comparison of the percentage distribution of expenditures in the two studies shows a marked divergence of spending habits, partly caused, perhaps, by local conditions and by shifts in relative prices since 1907, but attributable in great part to changes in wants and standards of living in the intervening twenty years. The Mexicans spent relatively less for food, housing, and fuel—the "necessaries" —and devoted nearly one-fourth of their total expenditure to those items which Chapin could afford to dismiss as "sundries," a category which includes the cost of an automobile, of all leisure-time and educational activities, association dues, charity, barber and cosmetics and personal cleaning supplies, furnishings, and all costs of operating the house other than fuel and light. This shift in the emphasis of expenditure exemplifies the changes which have occurred over this span of years. In 1907 the automobile was a new invention, purchased only by those with large incomes; by 1930 it was within the price range of one in every four Mexican workmen. In 1907 the radio had not yet been invented nor moving pictures perfected. The chief forms of recreation reported by the families in Chapin's study were excursions and lodge meetings. Many families reported no other form of recreation than visiting with relatives or neighbors. Twenty years later, low-priced radios were being bought on the installment plan, and the "talkies" had become the chief source of entertainment for all classes and ages, so much so that the majority of Mexican families spent for them more than $1 a month in addition to occasional patronage of other commercial amusements. Not only new inventions, but also the growth of installment selling and easy credit, the manufacturers' policy of developing new markets among the lower-income groups, and the effect of advertising in creating a demand for small luxuries, have all played their part in the changed direction of expenditure, which includes not only greater allowances for all forms of recreation, but also increased expenditures for furnishings, children's lessons, charities, and minor miscellaneous expenses.

The Mexicans obtained the surplus to spend on these "cultural" wants by reducing their proportional expenditures for food, housing, and fuel. Rents are higher in New York than in other parts of the country and more fuel is required on the Atlantic seaboard than in California. Although the New York families devoted a larger proportion of their total income to housing, overcrowding was as prevalent there as among the Mexicans, approximately half of each group falling below Chapin's standard of one and one-half persons per room. Housing conditions were probably better among the Mexicans, despite their lower proportional expenditure, because they escaped many of the evils attendant upon overcrowding by living in a small city almost suburban in character, with mild winters, and enjoyed the benefits of modern household conveniences and sanitation. It is important to remember that many conveniences which were seldom seen in 1907 had become common by 1929 —in particular, electricity and sanitary appliances. It is thus only to be expected that none of the families studied in 1907 had electricity and only three-fourths had gas for lighting, whereas 90 per cent of the Mexican dwellings were lighted by electricity; and only 18 per cent of the New York families had private baths and only 27 per cent had private toilets, in marked contrast to the 60 per cent and 70 per cent respectively among the Mexicans.

The New York families were better fed than the Mexicans. Chapin employed a standard to measure the adequacy of food expenditures which, after allowance is made for price changes, did not differ substantially from that used in the present study. He found 23 per cent of the New York families underfed, a contrast to 76 per cent of the Mexicans.

Data are lacking to make a direct comparison of the thriftiness of the two groups,[48] but apparently they made about the same provision for the future. Approximately three-fourths of both groups were paying life insurance premiums,[49] amounting to no more than burial insurance in the majority of cases, and about one-fourth reported savings for the year.

Chapin concludes that "an income of $900 or over probably permits the maintenance of a normal standard, at least so far as the physical man is concerned." The equivalent of the purchasing power of $900 in 1907 would be approximately $1600 in 1929–30. Only one Mexican family in four reported an income of this amount, yet the emphasis of Mexican spending was in the direction of those "higher wants," especially various forms of diversion, which are supposed to be a prerogative of much larger incomes.

---

[48] Since Chapin classified savings and investment as surplus, not as an item of expenditure, they have been omitted from the Mexican expenditures in table 31.

[49] This includes thirty-four families in the New York study and one in the Mexican which belonged to mutual benefit associations and therefore did not buy commercial insurance.

Homestead, Pennsylvania, 1907-8—mill hands.[50]—At the time when Chapin was studying the cost of living in New York, the Pittsburgh Survey of the Russell Sage Foundation was engaged in an investigation of the living conditions of steel workers in Homestead, Pennsylvania, in the course of which household accounts were collected from ninety families. Of these, 28 per cent were native white, 26 per cent Negro, 32 per cent Slav, and the remainder English, Scotch, Irish, and German immigrants. The average Homestead family was smaller by one child than the average Mexican family in the San Diego study. One family in five took in lodgers, contrasted to one family in fifty among the Mexicans.

The average weekly expenditure shown by the account books was $15.50,[51] the equivalent of $1400 per annum in 1929–30—about $50 a year higher than the average total expenditure of the Mexican families. No measure is available for difference in price levels resulting from difference of locality. Only 10 per cent of the wives were gainfully employed within the year. Families in which the man's earnings were low more commonly supplemented their income by taking lodgers.

As with the New York families, the principal difference in the distribution of expenditures of mill hands and Mexicans was the difference in emphasis on leisure-time activities and other secondary wants. This may result not only from those factors already considered in connection with the Chapin study, but also from the fact that the Homestead group was suffering at the time from under-employment and was forced to certain economies in its usual scale of living. The proportion spent on housing was the same in both groups; the Mexicans' relative allowance for food was slightly less. Since the Homestead families' real purchasing power was greater, especially with normal employment, there was less undernourishment and overcrowding. Applying the same standard food allowance as was used by Chapin, we find that 23 per cent of the Homestead families, the same proportion as in New York, were

[50] Byington, Margaret F., *Homestead*, Russell Sage Foundation (1910).
[51] Many of the accounts were kept during a period of depression and unemployment. The average family income per week was normally $18.

spending less than the minimum requirement for adequate nourishment. Of the Mexican families, 76 per cent fell below the Chapin standard. Fifty-six per cent of the Homestead families met the standard of at least one room per person, in contrast to 20 per cent of the Mexicans. As appeared in contrasting the New York families with the Mexicans, the developments of twenty years had greatly

TABLE 32

Percentage Distribution of Expenditures by Homestead
Mill Hands—Byington, 1907-8—Compared
with Mexicans

Item	Percentage of total expenditure excluding savings*	
	Homestead mill hands	San Diego Mexicans
Total expenditure	100.0	100.0
Food	40.7	37.6
Clothing	12.0	14.0
Housing	16.5	16.4
Fuel and light	4.1	2.7
Minor household expenses	2.5	3.1
Furnishings	2.1	2.7
Insurance	6.4	2.4
Medical care	2.4	2.1
Tobacco	0.4	1.2
Liquor	1.8	†
Other	11.1	17.8

* Regardless of the number of families reporting each item.
† The purchases of wine or beer reported in a few Mexican families were classified as food expenses. Probably some of the money reported as "incidentals" was spent for liquor.

improved sanitary conditions. Nearly half the Homestead families had no running water in the house; only one in six had an indoor water-closet; bathrooms were rare.

The mill families spent nearly three times as high a proportion of their income for insurance as did the Mexicans. This may be partly attributable to the fact that the men were engaged in a highly hazardous occupation in the days before workmen's compensation laws had been adopted.

United States, 1918–19—wage earners and small-salaried men.[52]—
The largest contemporary study in the field of cost of living was
made by the United States Bureau of Labor Statistics in 1918–19,
covering 12,096 families of wage earners and small-salaried men in
ninety-two cities. Seventy-five per cent of the inquiries covered the
calendar year 1918. It differed from the Mexican study in excluding
all families keeping boarders or having older children who paid
board, "slum" families, and non-English-speaking families which
had been less than five years in the country. Elimination of families
with older children who paid board and lodging naturally tended
to exclude the larger households. The average family contained five
persons, smaller by one-half person than the average Mexican
family in the present study.

The cost of living index of the Bureau of Labor Statistics showed
a decrease of 7 per cent between the years 1918[53] and 1929–30. The
average total expenditure in the government study, excluding
savings and investments which are listed as surplus, was $1434.
Corrected for the lower purchasing power of the dollar, the expenditures of the government families were no larger than those of the
average Mexican family (mean total expenditure $1348),[54] but there
were fewer mouths to feed. Less than 1 per cent of the average
income was derived from the earnings of the wives, in contrast
to 9 per cent in the average Mexican family.

The percentage distribution of expenditures shows a much closer
similarity to the Mexicans' spending habits than appeared in the
Chapin and Homestead studies. Expenditures for certain items
differ widely, but the emphasis on items other than food, clothing,
and shelter so characteristic of the Mexicans also appears in the
families studied in 1918–19.

---

[52] United States Bureau of Labor Statistics, Bulletin 357, *Cost of living in
the United States* (1924).

[53] The year covered by most of the schedules in the government study was
approximately the calendar year 1918. This and succeeding figures on changes
in the cost of living are taken from the United States Bureau of Labor Statistics index which appears semi-annually in the *Monthly Labor Review*.

[54] Excluding savings and investments.

TABLE 33

PERCENTAGE DISTRIBUTION OF EXPENDITURES BY WAGE-EARNERS' FAMILIES
IN THE UNITED STATES—UNITED STATES BUREAU OF LABOR STATISTICS,
1918–19—COMPARED WITH MEXICANS

Item	Percentage of total expenditure excluding savings*			
	United States wage earners		San Diego Mexicans	
Total expenditure	100.0		100.0	
Food	38.2		37.6	
Clothing	16.6		14.0	
Housing	13.0†		16.4	
House operation	7.6		5.8	
Fuel and light		5.2†		2.7
Other household expenses		2.4		3.1
Furnishings	4.5‡		2.7	
Care of person	1.0		2.6	
Automobile, motorcycle, bicycle	1.1		3.1	
Other transportation	1.9		1.9	
Insurance	3.0		2.4	
Medical care	4.2		2.1	
Leisure time	4.7		6.6	
Reading matter		0.7		0.4
Commercial amusements		0.8		1.7
Musical instruments		0.8		1.2
Vacation		0.5		0.3
Tobacco		1.2		1.2
Other		0.7		1.8
Associations	0.5		0.3	
Education	0.5		0.6	
School expenses		0.3		0.2
Lessons		0.2¶		0.4
Philanthropy	0.8§		1.1	
Church		0.7		0.3
Charity		0.1		0.1
Dependents		§		0.7
Other	1.8		2.8	

* Regardless of the number reporting each item.

† Three hundred and one families in which rent was combined with fuel and light are omitted.

‡ *Tools* have been added to the original class, "furnishings," and *musical instruments* moved to "leisure time."

¶ Only "music" is listed in the government study. Either no other types of lessons were purchased, or they have been included in "other miscellaneous."

§ Donations to dependents outside the home are apparently included in "gifts" which are classified under "leisure time—other."

TABLE 34

AVERAGE (MEAN) EXPENDITURE PER FAMILY REPORTING FOR CERTAIN SIG-
NIFICANT ITEMS BY WAGE-EARNERS' FAMILIES IN THE UNITED STATES—UNITED
STATES BUREAU OF LABOR STATISTICS, 1918–19—COMPARED WITH MEXICANS

Item	Percentage reporting		Mean annual expenditure per family reporting	
	United States wage earners	San Diego Mexicans	United States wage earners	San Diego Mexicans
Food	100	100	$548.51	$506.58
Clothing	100	100	237.60	188.50
Housing	*	98	186.55	225.57
Fuel and light	*	98	74.28	37.19
Cleaning supplies	100	100	12.15	20.88
Laundry sent out	70	59	17.91	24.54
Telephone	28	29	16.35	9.20
Service	16	8	25.04	24.00
Barber	96	95	7.87	14.44
Personal cleaning supplies	99	96	6.50	21.56
Automobile,motorcycle,bicycle	15	26	105.77	159.40
Carfare	89	98	27.02	20.60
Insurance	90	77	48.38	41.74
Doctor	86	56	37.33	27.67
Dentist	46	21	17.77	12.90
Hospital	11	6	42.76	60.83
Newspapers	96	52	8.17	7.98
Movies	78	82	10.07	18.07
Vacation	26	12	28.97	39.33
Tobacco	80	75	20.59	21.91
Union dues	31	30	14.93	7.96
Other association dues†	29	13	11.83	9.10
Music and other lessons‡	13	13	19.83	42.92
Church	72	62	14.15	6.06
Charity	30	51	4.49	2.48

* Two and one-half per cent of the families, where rent was combined with fuel and light, are
omitted.

† Lodge dues which were primarily insurance premiums were included under the latter
heading by the Bureau.

‡ See note, table 33.

Undernourishment, according to our standards, must have been
widely prevalent in the wage-earning class at the close of the war.
If food expenditures in the 1918–19 study are reduced to a 1929–
30 basis, the Mexicans, who were markedly underfed and whose

families were only slightly larger, spent slightly more for food. The Mexicans spent a higher proportion of their total budget on rent and reported more overcrowding, possibly because rents throughout the whole country increased 45 per cent from 1918 to 1929–30. The average 1918–19 family met the standard of one room per person. The characteristically high allowance of the Mexicans for leisure-time activities exceeded that of the average family in 1918–19. The average Mexican expenditure for commercial amusements was twice as large and musical instruments were more common, half of the purchases being radios, in contrast to pianos and phonographs ten years before. Nearly all the families studied in 1918–19 bought newspapers; only half the Mexicans, who also bought fewer magazines and books. Ownership of automobiles has, of course, tremendously increased since the war. Fifteen per cent of the families studied in 1918–19 owned automobiles, motorcycles, or bicycles. Twenty-six per cent of the Mexicans owned automobiles; one also had a bicycle. The Mexicans spent more on their cars.

The Mexicans made less provision for death, old age, or emergencies. Ninety per cent of the families studied in 1918–19 carried life or accident insurance, 77 per cent of the Mexicans. Savings and investments were classified as surplus in the earlier study, appearing in 70 per cent of the families and averaging $155 for each family reporting. Thirty-eight per cent of the Mexicans reported savings or investments, an average of $91 per family.

The families in the 1918–19 study spent 4 per cent of their budget on medical care, the Mexicans only 2 per cent. A greater proportion of families in the former study reported doctors' and dentists' bills. This may reflect, to some extent, the growth of free medical care in the intervening twelve years. Ninety-nine per cent of the 1918–19 families, however, reported expenditures for some sort of medical care, whereas 17 per cent of the Mexicans had no medical attention, either free or paid.

Oakland, California, 1924-25—street-car men.[55]—Five years previous to the present study the Heller Committee made a similar

---

[55] Heller Committee for Research in Social Economics, *Spending ways of a semi-skilled group*, Univ. Calif. Publ. Econ., 5 (1931): 295–366.

investigation of the incomes and expenditures of ninety-eight families of men employed on the local street and interurban electric railways and belonging to the Amalgamated Association of Street and Electrical Railway Employees.

The group was predominantly of native American and English-speaking stock. The average family in this group contained slightly more than two dependent children in contrast to the three or four children in the typical Mexican family investigated.[56] Twenty-two carmen's families reported boarders and lodgers, only two of the Mexican families. The street-car men's families included nine children who paid board.

The Bureau of Labor Statistics' cost of living index for San Francisco and Oakland showed practically no change between 1924–25 and 1929–30, so that the factor of shifting price levels may be disregarded in comparing the incomes of the two groups.[57]

The average income of street-car men's families was about $1800; the average Mexican family's income was about $1300. Only sixteen of the carmen's wives were employed within the year, forty-three of the Mexican women. The carmen's earnings formed a greater proportion of the total family income than did the earnings of Mexican men.

The percentage distribution of expenditure was strikingly similar in the two groups—37 per cent for food, 16 to 18 per cent for housing, 11 to 14 per cent for clothing, 6 per cent for house operation, and 3 per cent for furnishings, leaving one-fourth of the total expenditure for other items.

Since the Mexicans' total expenditure was only two-thirds as great as that of the street-car men and since their families were larger, the diversion of 25 per cent to secondary items left them obviously less well provided with necessaries. In the face of approximately equivalent food prices and an average family larger by 1.6 persons than the average carman's family, the Mexicans were

[56] The Mexican study excluded childless families, of which there were six among the street-car men.

[57] No figures are available for San Diego. It is impossible to measure the differences in living costs between the two localities, but it seems fair to assume that they are not very great.

TABLE 35

Average Expenditure per Family Regardless of the Number Reporting and Percentage Distribution of Expenditure by Oakland Street-car Men—Heller Committee, 1924–25—Compared with Mexicans

Item	Average annual expenditure per family		Percentage of total expenditure	
	Oakland street-car men	San Diego Mexicans	Oakland street-car men	San Diego Mexicans
Total expenditure	$2109.40	$1382.68	100.0	100.0
Food	790.65	506.58	37.5	36.6
Clothing	239.69	188.50	11.3	13.6
Men	$88.25	$52.02	4.2	3.8
Women	68.83	50.98	3.2	3.7
Children	82.03	83.45	3.9	6.0
Dependents	.58	2.05	.....	0.1
Housing	373.19	221.06	17.7	16.0
House operation	123.89	78.74	5.9	5.7
Light and fuel	75.05	36.44	3.6	2.6
Cleaning supplies	12.23*	20.88	0.6	1.5
Laundry sent out	19.82	14.48	0.9	1.1
Telephone	7.33	2.67	0.3	0.2
Other	9.46	4.27	0.5	0.3
Furniture and furnishings	74.32	36.42	3.5	2.6
Care of the person	33.42	34.42	1.6	2.5
Barber	13.43	13.72	0.6	1.0
Personal cleaning supplies	19.99	20.70	1.0	1.5
Leisure time	126.41	89.54	6.0	6.5
Reading matter	10.00	5.28	0.5	0.4
Commercial amusements	36.12	22.75	1.7	1.6
Vacations	25.32	4.72	1.2	0.4
Tobacco	17.59	16.43	0.8	1.2
Allowances to children	3.98	9.95	0.2	0.7
Gifts	26.15	6.03	1.2	0.4
Other	7.25	24.38	0.4	1.8
Automobile	55.85	41.26	2.7	3.0
Other transportation	23.64	25.78	1.1	1.9
Investments	110.46	66.81	5.2	4.8
Insurance	51.28	32.14	2.4	2.3
Investments and savings	59.18	34.67	2.8	2.5
Medical care	86.89	28.51	4.1	2.1
Associations	32.88	3.57	1.6	0.3
Unions	18.14	2.39	0.9	0.2
Other	14.74	1.18	0.7	0.1
Education	10.28	8.34	0.5	0.6
Tuition, supplies, etc.	5.82	2.76	0.3	0.2
Lessons	4.46	5.58	0.2	0.4
Charity	12.66	14.31	0.6	1.0
Dependents	4.10	9.29	0.2	0.6
Church	6.62	3.76	0.3	0.3
Charity	1.94	1.26	0.1	0.1
Other	15.17	38.84	0.7	2.8

* Thirty-three families were unable to separate these items from the total grocery bill.

spending nearly \$300 a year less for food. The available data indicate that only 4 per cent of the carmen's families were spending less than the standard allowance for food, in contrast to 76 per cent of

TABLE 36

AVERAGE (MEAN) EXPENDITURE PER FAMILY REPORTING FOR CERTAIN SIGNIFICANT ITEMS BY OAKLAND STREET-CAR MEN—HELLER COMMITTEE, 1924-25 —COMPARED WITH MEXICANS

Item	Number reporting		Mean annual expenditure per family reporting	
	Oakland street-car men	San Diego Mexicans	Oakland street-car men	San Diego Mexicans
House cleaning and laundry supplies	65*	100	\$ 18.44	\$ 20.88
Laundry sent out	58	59	33.49	24.54
Telephone†	34	29	21.12	9.20
Automobile	29	26	188.73	158.68
Insurance	89	77	56.47	41.74
Investments and savings	65	38	89.23	91.24
Reading matter	84	61	11.66	8.66
Commercial amusements	93	88	38.07	25.85
Vacation	24	12	103.40	39.33
Tobacco	62	75	27.80	21.91
Allowances to children	18	71	21.69	14.01
Gifts	89	56	28.69	10.77
Church	55	62	11.80	6.06
Charity	83	51	2.29	2.48
Dependents	6	33	67.00	28.15
School expenses, etc.	33	23	17.30	12.00
Lessons—music, etc.	11	13	39.68	42.92
Union dues	98	30	18.14	7.96
Other association dues	59	13	24.49	9.10

* The other families were unable to separate these items from the total grocery bill.
† Twenty-four street-car men's families and seven Mexicans had regular telephone service.

the Mexicans. Housing conditions among the Mexicans were notably poorer. Only one family in five achieved the standard of one room per person, which was met in two-thirds of the street-car men's families. Nearly half of the latter owned or were buying their homes, in contrast to 13 per cent of the Mexican families.

The Mexicans achieved great economies in the cost of fuel by gathering free wood; very few had telephones; otherwise, little difference is to be perceived in the costs of house operation for the two groups.

The Mexicans spent 6.5 per cent, $90, for leisure-time activities, the carmen 6 per cent, or $126. Of these items, vacations, gifts, and reading matter were more important in the budgets of the street-car men. Despite a lower income, as many Mexicans as street-car men owned automobiles,[58] and the costs were nearly as large.

Like most immigrants, the Mexicans had a greater burden of dependency. One-third contributed to the support of relatives, usually in Mexico. Only six of the ninety-eight street-car men reported such expenses.

As a group the carmen paid in full for their medical care; the Mexicans did not. This item amounted to 4 per cent of the average carman's budget, $87, and only 2 per cent, $29, for the average Mexican family.

The Mexicans were less well provided against death or economic disaster. Fewer families carried life insurance or saved money during the year, fewer belonged to unions or associations which might have benefit features, whereas every street-car man belonged at least to the union.

Chicago, 1924-25—unskilled laborers.[59]—Almost simultaneously with the Oakland study an investigation was made in Chicago of the incomes and standard of living of unskilled laborers as a check on the minimum budget in use by charitable agencies. These families were mainly immigrants; the majority were Poles or other Slavs and Italians. They differed from the San Diego Mexicans in having, on the average, only two or three dependent children instead of three or four, and in having fewer dependent relatives in the household.

---

[58] A study of the carmen in 1929–30 might show an increased proportion of automobile owners.

[59] Houghteling, Leila, *The income and standard of living of unskilled laborers in Chicago* (1927).

The median income of the Chicago families was $400 higher than the Mexicans',[60] $1674 as against $1274. Fewer wives were at work and more children were contributing to the family income. Unfortunately the method employed in this study does not permit a general comparison of the distribution of expenditures, but only of certain items.

Both smaller incomes and poorer dietary habits affected the Mexicans' food expenditures. Seventy-six per cent of the Mexican families fell below the standard allowance for food, and only 43 per cent of the Chicago families.[61] In both cases about one family in ten reported food expenditures more than 50 per cent below standard. The Chicago families spent 39 per cent of their total budget for food, the Mexicans only 37 per cent. A detailed analysis of the food purchases of a selected group of Chicago families showed that even when expenditures for food exceeded the standard, 63 per cent of the diets were inadequate in two, three, or four essentials. Examination of menus and of articles purchased makes it seem improbable that the twenty-two Mexican families which spent more than the standard allotment bettered this record.

The Mexicans likewise had less house room. Only 20 per cent reached or exceeded the standard of one room per person, in contrast to 33 per cent of the Chicago families. On the other hand, 78 per cent of the Mexicans had the use of a private bathroom, as against only 42 per cent of the Chicago families. Electricity for lighting was much more common in San Diego. Both groups spent about the same percentage of their total budget for rent. Twice as great a proportion of Chicagoans owned or were buying their homes, in spite of the greater size of the city.

Approximately the same proportion of families in both studies reported savings.

Detroit, 1929—Ford employees.[62]—Early in 1930 the United States Bureau of Labor Statistics made an investigation of the living con-

---

[60] As previously mentioned, there was no appreciable change in the cost of living between 1924–25 and 1929–30. No measure of the difference in living costs between Chicago and San Diego is available.

[61] The same food standard, adjusted to local prices, was used in both cases.

[62] "Standard of living of employees of the Ford Motor Co. in Detroit," *Monthly Labor Review*, XXX (1930): 1209–1252.

ditions and expenses of 100 Ford Motor Company employees in Detroit during 1929. Families included were limited to those in which the man worked at least 225 days in 1929 and earned approximately $7 a day, and in which there was no material income other than his earnings. The families included two or three children under sixteen, no older children, boarders, lodgers, or relatives, and had no outside dependents.

Because of the narrow limits set by these specifications, the average family consisted of 4.5 persons, of whom 2.5 were children under sixteen, and had an income of $1712, of which 99 per cent was the man's earnings. The average Mexican family in San Diego had one more child, and a number of families included older children or relatives. The average income of the Detroit group was $1712, or $375 a year more than the Mexicans' average. Nearly half the Mexican women were employed at some time in the year; families in which the woman was employed were excluded from the Detroit study.

The percentage distributions of expenditures by the two groups were closely similar, but there were greater differences than appeared between the Mexicans and the Oakland street-car men. Although any costs of purchasing a house which exceeded its rental value were classified as savings in the Detroit study, and thus excluded from expenditure, the proportion spent for housing by Ford employees was much greater than that spent by the Mexicans. The colder climate of Detroit necessitated much larger expenditures for fuel. The proportional expenditure for automobiles and for medical care was also greater in the Detroit study. The Mexicans, on the other hand, spent a much higher proportion of their total budget for leisure-time activities.

Analysis of the food purchases of the Ford employees indicated that "the food consumption of the Detroit families was, on the average, sufficient in quantity and well balanced as regards the important constituents of protein, calcium, phosphorus, and iron." Leaving out of consideration differences in price level between Detroit and San Diego,[63] the average Detroit family exceeded the

---

[63] No doubt such differences exist, but exact measures of them are lacking.

TABLE 37

Average Expenditure per Family Regardless of the Number Reporting and Percentage Distribution of Expenditure by Ford Employees in Detroit—United States Bureau of Labor Statistics, 1929—Compared with Mexicans

Item	Average annual expenditure per family		Percentage of total expenditure	
	Ford employees	San Diego Mexicans	Ford employees	San Diego Mexicans
Total expenditure*	$1719.83	$1348.01	100.0	100.0
Food	549.18	506.58	31.9	37.6
Clothing	210.67	188.50	12.2	14.0
Husband	63.59	52.02	3.7	3.9
Wife	59.21	50.98	3.4	3.8
Children	87.87	85.50†	5.1	6.3
Housing	390.59‡	221.06	22.7	16.4
House operation	136.56	78.74	7.9	5.8
Fuel and light	103.20	36.44	6.0	2.7
Cleaning supplies	16.64	20.88	1.0	1.5
Laundry sent out	4.23	14.48	0.2	1.1
Telephone	1.71	2.67	0.1	0.2
Service	1.08	1.92	0.1	0.1
Ice	6.94	.93	0.4	0.1
Moving	2.06	1.28	0.1	0.1
Other	.70¶	.14	......	......
Furnishings	76.05	36.42	4.5	2.7
Care of the person	26.05	34.42	1.5	2.5
Barber	12.37	13.72	0.7	1.0
Cleaning supplies	13.68	20.70	0.8	1.5
Leisure time	61.82	89.54	3.6	6.6
Movies	5.55	14.82	0.3	1.1
Other commercial amusements	1.09	7.93	0.1	0.6
Newspapers	12.06	4.15	0.7	0.3
Other reading matter	1.66	1.13	0.1	0.1
Radios—payments	6.26	11.59	0.4	0.9
Upkeep and other musical instruments	6.24	4.28	0.4	0.3
Vacation	2.59	4.72	0.1	0.3
Tobacco	19.08	16.43	1.1	1.2
Gifts	5.66§	6.03	0.3	0.4
Stationery and postage	1.63	2.59	0.1	0.2
Other	....	15.87	......	1.2
Automobile	76.78	41.26	4.5	3.1
Other transportation	41.08	25.78	2.4	1.9
Carfare	37.40	20.19	2.2	1.5
Travel	3.32	5.41	0.2	0.4
Bicycles	.36	.18	......	......

* Excluding savings and investments.

† Including eight dependent relatives for whom clothing was purchased.

‡ The excess of owners' payments over rental value of the house (av. $137) has been classified as savings. Garage rent has been included here.

¶ Property insurance only.

§ Presents of money to relatives are classified with gifts.

TABLE 37—(*Continued*)

Item	Average annual expenditure per family				Percentage of total expenditure			
	Ford employees		San Diego Mexicans		Ford employees		San Diego Mexicans	
Insurance—life and accident	$59.64		$32.14		3.5		2.4	
Medical care	64.23		28.51		3.7		2.1	
Doctor		38.17		15.49		2.2		1.1
Dentist		10.74		2.71		0.6		0.2
Drugs		8.99		4.81		0.5		0.4
Hospital		4.80		3.65		0.3		0.3
Other		1.53		1.85		0.1		0.1
Association dues	1.05‖		3.57		0.1		0.3	
Education	9.02		8.34		0.5		0.6	
School expenses		6.41		2.76		0.4		0.2
Lessons		2.61		5.58		0.1		0.4
Charity	11.15		14.31		0.7		1.1	
Dependents	**		9.29		......		0.7	
Church		9.62		3.76		0.6		0.3
Charitable agencies		1.53		1.26		0.1		0.1
Miscellaneous	5.96		38.84		0.3		2.9	

‖ None of these men belonged to unions.

** Families with dependent relatives were excluded from the study.

Nesbitt standard allowance used in the present study by 15 per cent. Moreover, the Ford employees apparently spent their food allowance more wisely than did the Mexicans, with a greater emphasis on milk products, fruit, vegetables, and meat, and less emphasis on dry groceries.

The Detroit families were better housed as well as better fed. The average family occupied a separate house of four or five rooms, one room per person, whereas the Mexicans with an average of one more person per family lived in a three- or four-room house. The average annual rent in Detroit was nearly twice as great, $391 as against $213 in San Diego. Bathrooms were equally common in both studies. Thirty-two of the Ford employees were buying their houses, in contrast to thirteen of the Mexicans.

The man and wife in the average Detroit family spent slightly more for clothing than did the Mexicans, but their wardrobes, replacements, and prices were strikingly similar. The Ford employees were a trifle better dressed, since the man's suits and shirts, the woman's dresses and hats, were replaced a little more frequently, but the basic wardrobes were practically identical.

The average Mexican family with an income $375 a year less than the average Detroit family spent actually more on amusements ($90 Mexicans, $62 Detroit). It spent more than three times as much for movies and commercial amusements. In Detroit it was chiefly the children who patronized movies, but this was not true of the Mexicans. Nearly twice as many of the Mexicans were buying radios. Every Detroit family took a newspaper, but only half the Mexicans.

The Mexicans' bill for toilet supplies and cosmetics was larger. Fifty-nine Mexican families sent out laundry at some time in the year, in contrast to twenty-two of the Detroit families.

Forty-seven of the Ford employees owned an automobile, and only twenty-six of the Mexicans. A greater number of Detroit families carried life insurance and the premiums were larger. Thirty-seven of the Detroit families managed to save an average of $134 during the year; twenty-five Mexican families saved an average of $109. Practically every Detroit family had some bill for medical care and the average bill was more than twice as large as that of the average Mexican family. The average Detroit purchase of furniture and furnishings was more than twice as large as that in San Diego.

One-third of the Mexican families were making some contribution to relatives outside the household. All families with dependents were excluded from the Detroit study.

With the exception of the allowance for dependents, the general scheme of expenditure of the Ford employees, so far as it differs from that of the Mexicans, is that of a more settled group, better fed, better housed, better prepared against catastrophe, probably paying all their doctors' bills, and spending less for amusements and the more frivolous items of expenditure.

Mexico, 1930—government employees.[64]—In 1930 the Oficina de Estudios Económicos of the Mexican National Railroads undertook to examine the living costs of employees of the Department of

[64] Ferrocarriles Nacionales de México, Oficina de Estudios Económicos, *Un estudio del costo de la vida en México*, Estudio número 2, Serie A.

the Treasury, who might be considered representative not only of all government office workers with similar salaries but of the whole Mexican middle class. For purposes of comparison with the San Diego study we shall consider only those groups of families[65] with three to five and six to eight members whose total income amounted to 1200–1800 pesos, or approximately \$480–\$720, the groups which most closely approach the San Diego Mexicans in size of family and of income, when the relative cost of living of the two countries is taken into consideration. Comparison has also been limited to results from the Distrito Federal, which included half the cases in the whole study. Where data were not classified by income and size of family, the results for all families studied in the district have been cited as being at least suggestive.

Comparison with this study does not, unfortunately, provide a contrast between the manner of living of the Mexican families in San Diego and the way they would live if they were at home, since it deals with the middle class instead of low-skilled wage earners. It indicates, however, the similarities and differences in expenditure between a standard of living in Mexico higher than working-class families could expect to reach and the standard which American wage scales enable them to maintain in this country.

The percentage distribution of expenditure[66] in the two groups shows two notable differences—a much smaller relative expenditure for food by the San Diego Mexicans, and the expenditure of an appreciable proportion of their income for items which would not occur in a working-class family budget in Mexico. The Mexican government employees devoted half or more of their total expenditure, depending on the size of family, to food; San Diego families about one-third. The proportion spent for clothing was about the same in both groups. The middle-class Mexicans at home spent 3

---

[65] By definition in this study, "family" included all members of the household except servants. No information was given on the composition of the average family or the number of wage earners. The average household in the Heller Committee study contained six persons.

[66] The classification used is that of the Oficina de Estudios Económicos. Greater detail was not available for that study. The absence of exact information on the relative costs of living in Mexico and in the United States made it seem inadvisable to attempt a comparison of actual monetary expenditures.

TABLE 38

Percentage Distribution of Expenditures by Mexican Government
Employees, 1930, Compared with San Diego Mexicans

Item	Percentage of total expenditure*		
	Mexican government employees		San Diego Mexicans
	Families of 3-5	Families of 6-8	
Total expenditure	100.0¶	100.0¶	100.0†
Food	50.1	57.0	37.6
Clothing	12.2	11.3	14.0
Housing	14.2‡	11.1‡	16.4
House operation and furnishings	7.9§	7.1§	8.5
Culture and diversions	4.9	4.6	3.0
(movies and theaters, excursions, education, reading matter, organization dues)			
Extraordinary expenses	2.9‡	3.0‡	8.3
(medical, taxes, insurance premiums, repairs to owned house, travel, automobile)			
Personal expenses	7.8	5.9	5.2
(tobacco, transportation—not journeys—barber, personal cleaning supplies, expenditures in *cantinas*)			
Other	....	....	7.0
(radios and other musical instruments, gifts, stationery and postage, miscellaneous leisure-time activities, charity, miscellaneous)			

* Regardless of number reporting.

¶ The percentage distribution, given in terms of income in the original study has been recomputed on the basis of total expenditure to agree with the Heller Committee study.

† Excluding savings and investments.

‡ Fire insurance, taxes, and repairs to house, which are classified under housing in Heller Committee studies, are here included under extraordinary expenses.

§ Costs of telephone, moving, and purchases of furniture other than bed linen, china, etc., were accidentally omitted from the schedule.

per cent for "extraordinary expenses," of which 2 per cent went to
the doctor, but the working-class Mexicans in San Diego spent over
8 per cent for this group of items, of which 3 per cent was for auto-

mobiles—26 per cent of the San Diego Mexicans owned cars, only 2.6 per cent of all the government employees in the Distrito Federal, including the highest incomes[67]—and 2.4 per cent for life insurance. Seven per cent of the average San Diego budget was spent on items which do not appear in the Mexico study, some accidentally omitted from the schedule, others, like radios, miscellaneous amusements, and support of dependents in the old country, characteristic of life in the United States. Although the San Diego Mexicans were of the working class and the government employees of Mexico represented the middle class, home-owning was more common among the former. Thirteen per cent of the San Diego Mexicans owned or were buying their homes, only 10 per cent of all income groups in the Distrito Federal; and this is probably a higher proportion than would be found in the Mexican middle class as a whole because of the facility for borrowing from the government pension fund.

The average government employee's family showed a considerable deficit between income and expenditure. According to the report, a large part of this was genuine and not due to errors of estimation. The deficit was probably explained by loans from more fortunate relatives and friends, unpaid rent, debts that run on forever, and graft money. The Mexicans in San Diego, with fewer credit resources, had fewer debts and deficits.

The government employees' budgets showed certain expenditures peculiar either to the social group or to Mexican life as contrasted with life in this country. Nearly 2 per cent of the average budget was spent for organization dues, because public employees were obliged to contribute a week's earnings each year to the Partido Nacional Revolucionario. Dues to all organizations cost the San Diego families 0.3 per cent a year. The other items included in the category "culture and diversions"—movies, education costs, reading matter, etc.—constituted about the same share of the family budget in both groups.

---

[67] The figure for the group with incomes of 1200–1800 pesos would undoubtedly have been even smaller.

In the smaller families in Mexico in which there was some surplus, expenditures for the category "personal expenses" were appreciably larger than among the San Diego Mexicans. This probably results from the item "expenditures in *cantinas.*"

In general, the chief differences between the budgets of middle-class Mexicans at home and emigrant working-class Mexicans appear to be that the latter spent proportionately much less for food and more for distinctively American secondary expenses such as automobiles and radios.

CASE HISTORIES

The following six individual budgets are appended to illustrate by direct example the spending habits and family circumstances within this group of Mexican families. The examples selected include: (1) the details of a poverty standard for a day laborer with four young children, who was employed only forty weeks in the year; (2), (3), (4) three families with incomes of $2000 or more, differing greatly among themselves, one clinging to Mexican customs, one a modern, Americanized young couple, and the third a large family supported chiefly by the earnings of the older children; (5) a fisherman's family of eight, reported to live in typical Mexican fashion; and (6) a family selected as expressing the group average in size, income, and distribution of expenditure.

1. Family Number 6

The man, forty-seven years old, and the wife, thirty-eight, were both born in Mexico, as were the two eldest daughters, aged nine and seven; the two youngest, three years and eight months old respectively, were born in California. The man spoke and read English; the wife did not.

This family was living in poverty. Six persons were dependent on the man's earnings during forty weeks of the year as a day laborer, amounting to $748. They were overcrowded and undernourished and had little else than bare necessities.

Although one-half of the family budget went for food, the expenditure was far below minimum standard requirements. It was supplemented to some extent by discarded fish from the boats. Tortillas were served twice a day, frijoles always at lunch and often at dinner. The latter meal usually consisted of meat, fish or eggs, and one vegetable, usually potatoes. Nearly 30 per cent of the food allowance was spent for milk.

The flat, renting for $9 a month, contained three rooms for five people and a baby, no bathroom, an outside water-closet shared by three families.

FAMILY NUMBER 6

INCOME

Total income....$748.00	Man's earnings........$748.00	Reported deficit, $11.09 (error of estimation)

EXPENDITURE

Item	Amount		Percentage	
Total expenditure............................	$ 759.09		100.0	
Food (meals at home)............................	380.64*		50.1	
Clothing................................	111.95		14.8	
Man................................		$34.35		4.5
Wife................................		27.00		3.6
Children (4)................................		50.60		6.7
Rent................................	108.00†		14.2	
House operation................................	59.50		7.8	
Electricity and gas................................		33.70‡		4.4
Cleaning and laundry supplies...................		25.80		3.4
Care of the person (barber for man).............	4.20		0.6	
Furnishings................................	30.00		4.0	
Sewing machine................................		28.00		3.7
Minor items................................		2.00		0.3
Leisure time................................	21.80		2.9	
Amusements (not specified)........................		6.00		0.8
Tobacco................................		7.80		1.0
Spending money for children........................		8.00		1.1
Transportation (carfare)............................	10.00		1.3	
Medical care (man)................................	33.00¶		4.3	

* 37.3 per cent below standard.   ‡ Wood free.
† Includes water costs.   ¶ Other medical service free.

The family purchased, within the year of this study, a sewing machine, a profitable investment, since the mother made most of the family garments. She and the husband purchased almost complete outfits of clothing for $34 and $27 respectively. The children's shoes cost $1 a pair, and other articles were purchased on the same price scale.

Costs of house operation were limited to electricity, gas, and laundry soap and supplies. There was no household service, nor any laundry sent out, even though a child was born. The family bought no toothbrushes, no toothpaste, toilet soap, drugs, cosmetics, or shaving supplies, depending entirely on laundry soap for their personal cleansing.

The man spent $33 for a doctor when good advice would have sent him to a clinic. The mother must have received free care when the child was born, although none was reported. The older children were innoculated against diphtheria by the school nurse.

The family went to no movies, unless the tickets were purchased out of the children's spending money, and spent within the year only $6 for other amusements.

There was no provision for the future, neither insurance nor savings, but the family was not in debt.

2. FAMILY NUMBER 100

The family consisted of the father, thirty-one years old, the mother, aged twenty-eight, a boy of ten, girls of nine and seven, and the wife's semi-dependent parents, forty-six and forty-four years old, all born in Mexico.

This family represents the successful immigrants who have made money in the new country without making any very radical change in their standards of living. The man was a contracting brick-mason whose net profits were $2500 in 1929–30, the highest income of any family in the study. Nevertheless, the allotment for food was 37 per cent less than the minimum standard, and the house which they were purchasing had been converted into such as "might be found among the middle class any where in Spanish-speaking America," with a high-fenced yard in which were a vegetable garden, chickens, a goat, a kettle for boiling water, and a pile of firewood. "Everything was orderly and clean, with a decidedly exotic air." With a comfortable income they did not use their surplus to get better food or to lighten the woman's household duties by occasional domestic service or laundry sent out.

FAMILY NUMBER 100

INCOME

Total income..$2500.00	Man's earnings......$2500.00	Reported surplus $6.70
		Cash on hand...... 20.00
		Error of estimation.................... 13.30

EXPENDITURE

Item	Amount		Percentage	
Total expenditure................................	$2493.30		100.0	
Food..	608.00		24.4	
Meals at home................................		$520.00*		20.9
Meals bought (husband)................		40.00		1.6
Grapes for wine............................		20.00		0.8
Sweets, etc., for fiestas................		10.00		0.4
Feed for chickens and goat..........		18.00		0.7
Clothing..	302.00		12.1	
Man..		99.75		4.0
Wife..		83.40		3.3
Children (3)................................		118.85		4.8
Housing (purchasing)......................	729.00		29.3	
Installments and interest..............		640.00		25.7
Taxes and assessments..................		65.00		2.6
Water..		14.00		0.6
Repairs..		10.00		0.4
House operation..............................	35.50		1.4	
Electricity....................................		18.00†		0.7
Cleaning and laundry supplies......		17.50		0.7
Care of the person..........................	37.00		1.5	
Barber (man and children)............		18.00		0.7
Personal cleaning supplies............		19.00		0.8
Furnishings (minor items)................	6.00		0.2	
Leisure time....................................	135.00		5.4	
Movies (4 persons)........................		24.00		1.0
Pool and billiards..........................		20.00		0.8
Newspaper....................................		12.00		0.5
Tobacco..		26.00		1.0
Tuning piano................................		10.00		0.4
Spending money for children........		23.00		0.9
Gifts..		15.00		0.6
Other (stationery, magazines)......		5.00		0.2
Automobiles (2)—upkeep..............	353.00		14.1	
Transportation (carfare)................	12.00		0.5	
Investments....................................	159.80		6.4	
Insurance (5 persons)....................		59.80‡		2.4
Bank savings................................		100.00		4.0
Medical care (at clinic)..................	54.00		2.2	
Associations (union dues)..............	9.00		0.4	
Education (music lessons)..............	16.00		0.6	
Charity..	37.00		1.5	
Dependents (sister-in-law in Mexico)........		25.00		1.0
Church..		12.00		0.5

* 36.8 per cent below standard, but this deficiency is mitigated to some extent by garden produce, chickens and eggs, and goat milk, not included in cash expenditure.

† Wood free.   ‡ $26 for man.

It is impossible on an income of $2500 completely to safeguard a family against the economic consequences of the wage-earner's death. These people with equity in a house, bank savings, and probably $1000 life insurance for the man were far better off than most of their compatriots.

They had adopted American working-class standards of dress; they owned two cars, one partly for business purposes; they patronized movies and poolrooms, gave the children spending money and music lessons, sent small sums to a relative in Mexico—lived, in short, according to their own ideas of comfort, if not luxury.

3. FAMILY NUMBER 93

The parents, twenty-eight and twenty-four years old, were born in Mexico, the two children, three and two years old, in California.

This family, also enjoying an income far above the average, was a direct contrast to Number 100 in its spending ways. "This is an up-to-date young couple . . . . in a furnished apartment; they seem to have all modern comforts." The man worked in an office as commission agent, at $150 a month, and the wife also did office work for part of the year, leaving the children at a day nursery. Both parents could read and write English. The family lived in a two-room furnished apartment, with a private bathroom, gas, hot-water heater, electricity—the very antithesis of the back-yard pile of driftwood, and the kettle of frijoles common to most families of the study.

Their food allowance gave a comfortable margin over the minimum standard, although it is impossible to tell how wisely they spent it. Their laundry was sent out regularly. The man, as an office worker, was required to dress better than a manual laborer, but his $185 clothing budget, including two $5 hats, a $35 overcoat and a $40 suit, $20 for shoe shines, and other items to scale, represented some degree of luxury above the minimum requirements of neatness. The woman's wardrobe, although of cheaper quality, was also above the minimum. She spent $8 for cosmetics.

Nearly 10 per cent of the family budget went into leisure-time activities—movies once a week, entertaining friends, purchasing a

FAMILY NUMBER 93

INCOME

Total income..$2016.00	Man's earnings......$1800.00	Reported deficit $25.15
	Wife's earnings...... 216.00	(error of estimation)

EXPENDITURE

Item	Amount		Percentage	
Total expenditure	$2041.15		100.0	
Food	600.50		29.4	
Meals at home		$520.00*		25.4
Meals bought (husband's lunches)		62.50		3.1
Beverages, etc		18.00		0.9
Clothing	388.15		19.0	
Man		184.50		9.0
Wife		132.50		6.5
Children (2)		71.15		3.5
Rent (furnished apartment)	307.50†		15.1	
House operation	91.30		4.5	
Gas and kerosene		29.00		1.4
Telephone tolls		12.00		0.6
Cleaning and laundry supplies		12.80		0.6
Laundry (every 2 weeks)		26.00		1.3
Moving		11.50		0.6
Care of the person	51.10		2.5	
Barber (whole family)		22.00		1.1
Personal cleaning supplies and cosmetics		29.10		1.4
Leisure time	198.00		9.7	
Movies (parents)		35.00		1.7
Pool and billiards		15.00		0.7
Installments on radio		50.00		2.4
Tobacco		52.00		2.6
Social entertainment		15.00		0.7
Magazines		3.00		0.2
Photographs and toys		18.00		0.9
Stationery and stamps		10.00		0.5
Transportation	35.00‡		1.7	
Carfare		20.00		1.0
Travel		15.00		0.7
Investments	280.60		13.8	
Insurance (3 persons)		40.60		2.0
Bank savings		120.00		5.9
Investments (real estate)		120.00		5.9
Medical care (dentist)	18.00		0.9	
Education (day nursery)	25.00		1.2	
Charity	26.00		1.2	
Dependents (mother in Mexico)		25.00		1.2
Charity		1.00		....
Incidentals	20.00		1.0	

* Exceeds standard by 32.5 per cent.   ‡ Use of company car for Sunday excursions, etc.
† Includes electricity and water costs.

radio, $1 a week for tobacco, etc. The family had the use of the firm's automobile for excursions and picnics. The absence of automobile upkeep costs partly explains why these people could live in comfort, have their pleasures, and still invest 14 per cent of their income in insurance, bank savings, and real estate. An additional factor was the smallness of the family—two children instead of the average three or four.

4. Family Number 95

This family consisted of a father, aged forty-five, a mother, thirty-five, four girls of twenty, fifteen, thirteen, and ten, and two boys of nineteen and seventeen, all born in California.

This family had an income of over $2000, but it meant very much less in terms of well-being than in the case of two families already described, since the father's earnings constituted only one-third of the total income, the chief source being the earnings of the three eldest children, seventeen to twenty years old, and the mother. The income, therefore, had to care for the needs of a family of eight, three of whom were grown children with the responsibilities and demands of adults.

The father was a carpenter, employed only sixteen weeks in the year; the mother and eldest daughter worked half-time in the cannery for thirty-two weeks; the two boys were employed as mechanics' helpers for twenty-six and sixteen weeks, respectively. All the children turned their total earnings into the family purse and received back $1 a month for spending money.

The food allowance was 29 per cent below standard, not far from the average for the group. All meals were eaten at home or carried to work. The sample menus for two days included tortillas, frijoles, soup, and meat.

By the standards used in this study the family was adequately housed. For $23 a month it rented a six-room house with electricity, bathroom, and water-closet, and three bedrooms. No description of the condition of the house was given in the schedule.

The clothing bill was unusually large—one-fifth of the whole budget—because of the demands of five children in their 'teens.

FAMILY NUMBER 95

INCOME

Total income..$2036.40	Man's earnings......$768.00	Reported deficit..$96.00
	Wife's earnings...... 288.00	(error of estimation)
	Girl 20, earnings.... 288.00	
	Boy 19, earnings.... 390.00	
	Boy 17, earnings.... 158.40	
	Rental...................... 144.00	

EXPENDITURE

Item	Amount		Percentage	
Total expenditure...	$2132.40		100.0	
Food...	786.80		36.9	
Meals at home........................		$774.80*		36.3
Feed for chickens........................		12.00		0.6
Clothing........................	421.60		19.8	
Man........................		38.00		1.8
Wife........................		56.60		2.7
Working children (3)...............................		181.50		8.5
Younger children (3)...............................		145.50		6.8
Rent........................	276.00†		12.9	
House operation........................	108.40		5.1	
Electricity and kerosene...........................		54.00		2.6
Telephone—12 months...............................		39.00		1.8
Cleaning and laundry supplies...................		15.40		0.7
Care of the person........................	35.80		1.7	
Barber (man and children)........................		14.40		0.7
Personal cleaning supplies and cosmetics		21.40		1.0
Furnishings........................	118.00		5.5	
Installments (washing and sewing machines)........................		95.00		4.5
Curtains and bed linen...............................		20.00		0.9
Minor items........................		3.00		0.1
Leisure time........................	78.80		3.7	
Movies (5 persons)...............................		20.00		0.9
Radio installments........................		10.00		0.5
Newspaper........................		10.80		0.5
Spending money for 3 oldest children.......		36.00		1.7
Stationery and stamps...............................		2.00		0.1
Automobile—upkeep........................	212.00		10.0	
Transportation (carfare)...............................	5.00		0.2	
Insurance (man—20-year endowment).........	21.00.		1.0	
Medical care (at clinic)...............................	30.00		1.4	
Dentist........................		25.00		1.2
Drugs........................		5.00		0.2
Education........................	15.00		0.7	
School books........................		5.00		0.2
Music lessons........................		10.00		0.5
Charity (church)........................	24.00		1.1	

* 29.1 per cent below standard; supplemented by a few home-grown vegetables, chickens, and eggs.
† Includes water costs.

The family's habits of spending inclined toward many very cheap articles. The eldest girl, for example, bought three hats at $1, two coats at $10, three dresses at $5, and three pairs of shoes at $3.50. Each of the three elder girls bought, within the year, 10 pairs of silk stockings at $1 or less.

The largest single item after food, clothing, and rent was the cost of running the family automobile, $212 a year, or 10 per cent of the total income. The next was furnishings, 5.5 per cent, which included $95 in installments on a washing machine and a sewing machine. Installments on a radio amounted to $10. The fuel bill was large, because all cooking was done on a kerosene stove. This was one of the seven families having a telephone.

The proportionate share of most of the other items was below average. This was notably true of leisure-time activities, for which the automobile was probably an alternative, provision for the future, which was limited to a small insurance policy for the man, and bills for dental care at a clinic.

5. Family Number 50

The father, twenty-eight years old, the mother, twenty-six, and the two elder girls, aged seven and six, were born in Mexico. The younger girls, four and three years old, and the baby boy of six months, were born in California. The household also included the wife's elder sister, who paid board and lodging and helped with household tasks.

The family was selected because it was described by the investigator as living in typical Mexican country style, so far as it can be transplanted to an alien environment.

The father was a fisherman, frequently absent on trips. His earnings, a percentage of the profits, were irregular, but probably averaged $20 a week throughout the year. When at home, he supplemented the food purchased by fish and other produce from the wharfs. The family never bought meat. Because of the man's absences it was impossible to determine the cost of a standard diet for this family. The expenditure for food was almost certainly below standard.

The family of eight lived in a four-room house at the rear of a vacant lot, renting for $15 a month. It had electricity, a water-closet on the porch, no bathroom, and no gas. Cooking was done with driftwood. The women ground their own meal for tortillas in a stone metate and baked the cakes on an iron plate over an open fire in the yard, exactly as if they were living in Mexico. The investigator reported: "their ideas of cleanliness and order are at least primitive."

The allowance for clothing was low, especially the $5 allowance for each of the younger children. But the children wore few clothes at home, the family received some gifts of clothing, and the mother was clever at making and remodeling.

The proportion spent for "necessaries" was below average; the unusually heavy items of expense were furnishings, medical care, savings, and amusements. The family had no automobile. During the year the family paid $30 in installments on a sewing machine, $35 for a bed and dresser, and $17 for other furnishings. The doctor and drug bills at the clinic were low, but the mother's two weeks in the hospital when the baby was born cost $75. In addition to $65 in premiums for small insurance policies for the parents and four older children, they saved $150, $80 of which was withdrawn to meet hospital expenses. Nine per cent of the budget, $121, was spent on leisure-time activities—movies about twice a month for the parents, $28 a year for other commercial amusements for the man, 50 cents a week for tobacco, 10 cents a week for chewing gum, 15 cents a week for the children's spending money. They bought a phonograph, and took a vacation visiting relatives on a farm below Tia Juana, which cost nothing but bus fare and spending money. In addition, $20 a year was reported for the husband's miscellaneous expenses.

The family afforded an excellent example of a standard of food, clothing, and housing which had not risen with income and therefore left a large surplus, half the total, for expenditure in other directions.

FAMILY NUMBER 50

Income

| Total income..$1280.00 | Man's earnings......$1040.00
Sister-in-law's
    contributions...   240.00 | Reported deficit $68.75
Drawn from sav-
    ings.................... 80.00
Error of estima-
    tion...................... 11.25 |

Expenditure

Item	Amount	Percentage
Total expenditure...	$1348.75	100.0
Food...	376.65	27.9
Meals at home...	$364.65*	27.0
Feed for chickens..	12.00	0.9
Clothing...	141.10†	10.5
Man...	34.50	2.6
Wife...	44.40	3.3
Children (5)...	62.20	4.6
Rent...	180.00‡	13.3
House operation...	30.80	2.3
Electricity...	10.80§	0.8
Cleaning and laundry supplies.....................	14.00	1.1
Laundry while wife was in hospital.............	6.00	0.4
Care of the person..	41.50	3.1
Barber (whole family).................................	19.00	1.4
Personal cleaning supplies...........................	22.50	1.7
Furnishings...	82.00	6.1
Installments on sewing machine...................	30.00	2.2
Bed and dresser..	35.00	2.6
Linoleum and blankets..................................	10.00	0.8
Minor items..	7.00	0.5
Leisure time..	120.70	8.9
Vacation (family, 1 week).............................	18.00¶	1.3
Movies (2 persons).......................................	15.00	1.1
Pool and billiards...	12.00	0.9
Sports events..	6.00	0.4
Games of chance...	10.00	0.8

* The father was so frequently absent on fishing trips that it was impossible to compute the number of equivalent adult males fed during the year. The cash expenditure was supplemented by eggs and rabbits, and by fish and other food from the boats.

† The sister-in-law paid for her clothing and all other expenses except board and room.

‡ Includes water costs.   § Wood free.

¶ Bus fare and spending money; visited relatives across the border.

FAMILY NUMBER 50—(*Continued*)

EXPENDITURE—(*Continued*)

Item	Amount		Percentage	
Leisure time—(*Continued*)				
Phonograph		$ 15.00		1.1
Tobacco		26.00		1.9
Chewing gum		5.20		0.4
Gifts		4.00		0.3
Spending money for children		7.50		0.6
Stationery and stamps		2.00		0.1
Transportation (carfare)	$ 12.00		0.9	
Investments	215.00		15.9	
Insurance (6 persons)		65.00		4.8
Savings		150.00		11.1
Medical care	97.00		7.2	
Doctor (clinic)		12.00		0.9
Drugs (clinic)		10.00		0.8
Hospital		75.00		5.5
Charity	32.00		2.4	
Dependents (father in Mexico)		20.00		1.5
Church		12.00		0.9
Incidentals (husband)	20.00		1.5	

6. FAMILY NUMBER 32

The father, twenty-eight years old, the mother, twenty-six, a girl of eight, and a boy of six were born in Mexico. The younger children, a boy of four and a girl of two, were born in California.

This family was chosen as the best example of the "average family." The parents were born in Mexico, and had been five years in this country. The wife could not read or write. The man read a little Spanish. There were four young children, and no other persons in the household. The father was employed as a laborer on a steady job with the gas company for forty-eight weeks of the year. His earnings constituted the entire family income, $1148, somewhat lower than the median for the group. The family had no automobile.

Expenditures for food and clothing were approximately average. The allowance for meals at home was 32.4 per cent below standard, but goat's milk, vegetables, and probably eggs from their hens, reduced, without entirely removing, the deficit. Home-made tortillas were served every day. The wife made many of the clothes for herself and the younger children. The man bought two hats in the year, two pairs of pants at $7, three overalls, six shirts at $2, two suits of underwear, twelve pairs of cheap socks, four pairs of shoes at $2.50, three ties at 50 cents, and spent $8 on shoe repairs and shines. The wife purchased three house dresses at $1, two better dresses at $3, four "corsets" at 50 cents, two suits of cheap underwear, six nightgowns, two pairs of silk stockings at 50 cents and four pairs of cotton at 25 cents, a pair of $4 shoes, and $2 worth of yard goods, probably for underwear, aprons, etc.

The family of six lived in a four-room house and slept in one room in two double beds. The large kitchen was used as a living room. Another room was set aside as the ceremonial "sala." The house was fitted with electricity, a bathroom, and a water-closet on the porch. Cooking was done with driftwood. The large back yard contained a shed for the goat, a patch of alfalfa, and a small vegetable garden. The house rented for $14 a month, not including water costs.

The costs of house operation were low, because no gas was used, although they included $20 for laundry sent out.

The father and the boy of six had their hair cut by the barber. The item of cleaning supplies was unusually low—two toothbrushes, six tubes of toothpaste, $4 for household drugs and antiseptics. Apparently the family washed and shaved with laundry soap and used no cosmetics.

The unusually high allowance for furnishings resulted from the purchase in ten installments during the year of a $65 living-room set for the "sala."

Eighteen per cent of the budget went for other items, chiefly movies, tobacco, and money sent to the man's mother in Mexico. The family went to the movies fifty times in the year. The man also spent $10 on pool and $39, twice the average allotment, for tobacco. The three elder children got 10 cents a week for spending money. Naturally, being illiterate, the adults bought no papers or magazines.

FAMILY NUMBER 32

INCOME

Total income, $1148.00	Man's earnings, $1148.00	Reported surplus $6.60 Unpaid bills.......... 10.00 Error of estima- tion.................... 16.60

EXPENDITURE

Item	Amount		Percentage	
Total expenditure..	$1141.40		100.0	
Food..	465.00		40.7	
Meals at home............................		$416.00*		36.4
Meals bought (child's lunches)................		16.00		1.4
Feed for goat and chickens.....................		33.00		2.9
Clothing..	151.60		13.3	
Man..		60.50		5.3
Wife..		22.70		2.0
Children (4).................................		68.40		6.0
Housing..	180.00		15.8	
Rent..		168.00		14.7
Water..		12.00		1.1
House operation............................	49.90		4.4	
Electricity............................		12.80†		1.1
Cleaning and laundry supplies................		17.10		1.5
Laundry (20 weeks)........................		20.00		1.8
Care of the person........................	16.50		1.4	
Barber (man and one boy)................		10.50		0.9
Personal cleaning supplies................		6.00		0.5
Furnishings..	76.00		6.6	
Living-room set............................		65.00		5.7
Blankets..		9.50		0.8
Minor items.................................		1.50		0.1
Leisure time....................................	94.60		8.3	
Movies (3 persons)........................		30.00		2.6
Pool and billiards........................		10.00		0.9
Tobacco..		39.00		3.4
Spending money for children................		15.60		1.4
Transportation (carfare).....................	7.00		0.6	
Insurance (4 children)........................	20.80		1.8	
Medical care (at clinic).....................	18.00		1.6	
Doctor (clinic)............................		6.00		0.5
Dentist (clinic)............................		4.00		0.4
Drugs (clinic)............................		8.00		0.7
Associations (union dues).....................	9.00		0.8	
Charity..	41.00		3.6	
Dependents (mother in Mexico)................		30.00		2.6
Church..		10.00		0.9
Charity..		1.00		0.1
Incidentals (husband)........................	12.00		1.1	

* 32.4 per cent below standard, but supplemented by milk from the goat for 40 weeks, a few vegetables, and probably eggs and chickens, which reduce the deficit.

† Wood free.

The family had no automobile, and no carfare to or from work or school. Provision for the future was limited to very small insurance policies on the four children. In spite of four young children in the family the bills for medical care, received at a clinic, were only $18 for the year.

APPENDICES

APPENDIX A

Clothing Details

A brief explanation of the derivation of the following tables seems desirable. The schedule called for an enumeration of the articles and cost of clothing bought for each member of the family during the year. It did not furnish any information about the stock of clothing already on hand, and without such information the wardrobe of different members of the average family could not be computed. Revisits to a number of families were planned in order to obtain inventories of the stock of clothing on hand. Clothing schedules were made up for persons of various age and sex groups—men, women, boys over twelve, girls over twelve, boys between two and twelve, girls between two and twelve, children under two. When an investigator was sent out in the fall of 1931, the shortage of funds made it necessary to limit the work to inventories for ten representatives of each of these seven groups. The investigator was instructed to select the individuals as far as possible from "typical" families of the earlier investigation. Upon the representative quality of this small sample depends the value of the column "stock" in the succeeding tables, and, to a less extent, the list of articles included.

As far as possible the tables include articles purchased by more than half the persons of the same age and sex group in the original study or appearing in more than half the wardrobes studied. The number of garments bought per year and the prices are based on the arithmetic average for all persons in the age and sex group; the unit price is based on the arithmetic average for persons reporting the article. The total annual cost in each case is close to the median for persons of that sex and age.

The results obtained from the two investigations were not wholly consistent. In the case of short-lived articles reported in the majority of wardrobes but purchased during the year by only a few persons of the original group, several explanations are possible. The group of ten reporting on their wardrobes may have had higher incomes and standards of dress. Articles such as handkerchiefs might have been gifts. Nightgowns and other garments might have been made from yard goods. Occasionally a new item had been added by a change in styles. Such articles were noted in the tables but no allowance made for replacement.

Another type of problem that arose was related to articles which might be substituted for each other, such as silk or cotton stockings. Frequently the balance of choices in the reports was so nearly equal that no true norm could be established, and the selection for inclusion in the "typical" wardrobe was necessarily arbitrary.

APPENDIX A 1

Stock and Annual Replacement of Clothing for a Man

Item	Stock on hand (base—10 persons)	Annual replacement	Unit price	Annual cost
		(base—100 families)		
Hat	1	½	$3.50	$1.75
Cap	1	⅓	1.75	.58
Lumberjacket*	....	....	....	....
Sweater	1	½	3.50	1.75
Suit	2†	¼†	26.00	6.50
Separate pants	2	1	3.50	3.50
Overalls	2	2	2.00	4.00
Shirts	4	4	1.15	4.60
Underwear	3	3	1.00	3.00
Nightclothes*	....	....	....	....
Socks	6	14	.25	3.50
Shoes	2	2½	4.50	11.25
Ties	2	1	1.00	1.00
Handkerchiefs	6	4	.15	.60
Garters*	....	....	....	....
Suspenders*	....	....	....	....
Belt	1	⅓	1.25	.42
Other items‡	....	....	....	
Total replacements	....	....	....	42.45
Shoe repairs	....	1	1.50	1.50
Total cost				**$43.95**

* This item appeared in half or more of the wardrobes studied, but few or no purchases appeared in the original schedules.

† The stock is apparently inconsistent with the replacement figures.

‡ More than half of the 10 men reporting on their wardrobes owned at least one additional minor item.

APPENDIX A 2

Stock and Annual Replacement of Clothing for a Woman

Item	Stock on hand (base—10 persons)	Annual replacement	Unit price	Annual cost
		(base—100 families)		
Hat	2	1	$2.25	$2.25
Coat	1	½	18.00	9.00
Sweater	1	⅕	2.50	.50
Skirt or suit*	....	....	....	....
Blouses*	....	....	....	....
House dresses	3	3	1.00	3.00
Other dresses	2	1	9.00	9.00
Aprons	4	1⅓	.75	1.00
Corsets—girdle	2†	½	2.00	1.00
Underwear	3	3	.75	2.25
Nightclothes	3	¾	1.00	.75
Silk stockings	‡	3½	1.00	3.50
Other stockings	‡	3½	.50	1.75
Shoes	3	2	4.50	9.00
Scarf*	....	....	....	....
Handkerchiefs*	....	....	....	....
Handbag	1	¼	2.00	.50
Yard goods	....	....	....	1.50
Other items¶	....	....	....	....
Total cost	....	....	....	$45.00

* This item appeared in half or more of the wardrobes studied, but few purchases appeared in the original schedules.

† The stock is apparently inconsistent with the replacement figures.

‡ Because silk and cotton stockings are alternatives but have different wearing value, the evidence of 10 cases was too scattered to be conclusive. Each type was purchased by two-thirds of the 100 women.

¶ More than half of the 10 women reporting on their wardrobes owned at least one additional minor item.

APPENDIX A 3

STOCK AND ANNUAL REPLACEMENT OF CLOTHING FOR A BOY 12 OR OLDER

Item	Stock on hand (base—10 persons)	Annual replacement	Unit price	Annual cost
		(base—100 families)		
Hat*	....	....	....	....
Cap	1	1	$1.00	$1.00
Sweater	1	1	2.75	2.75
Suit	1	½	20.00	10.00
Separate pants	2	1	2.75	2.75
Overalls	2	2	1.25	2.50
Shirts	4	4	.85	3.40
Underwear	3	2½	.80	2.00
Socks	6	11	.20	2.20
Shoes	2	3	3.25	9.75
Handkerchiefs*	....	....	....	....
Ties*	....	....	....	....
Belt	2	½	.80	.40
Suspenders*	....	....	....	....
Total cost	....	....	....	$36.75

* This item appeared in half or more of the wardrobes studied, but few purchases appeared in the original schedules.

APPENDIX A 4

STOCK AND ANNUAL REPLACEMENT OF CLOTHING FOR A GIRL
BETWEEN 2 AND 12 YEARS

Item	Stock on hand (base—10 persons)	Annual replacement	Unit price	Annual cost
		(base—100 families)		
Hat	1	⅓	$1.00	$ .33
Coat*	....	....	....	....
Sweater	2	¾	1.50	1.12
Skirt*	....	....	....	....
Middies*	....	....	....	....
School or house dresses	4	4	.75	3.00
Other dresses	1	½	2.00	1.00
Aprons*	....	....	....	....
Underwear	4	2½	.50	1.25
Nightclothes*	....	....	....	....
Socks	4	8	.25	2.00
Shoes	2	3½	2.50	8.75
Yard goods	....	....	....	1.50
Total cost	....	....	....	$18.95

* This item appeared in half or more of the wardrobes studied, but few purchases appeared in the original schedules.

APPENDIX B

AVERAGE EXPENDITURE PER FAMILY FOR SPECIFIED ITEMS REGARDLESS OF THE
NUMBER OF FAMILIES REPORTING SUCH EXPENDITURES

Items	Average expenditure per family	Percentage of total expenditure
All items	$1382.68	100.0
Food	506.58	36.6
Housing	221.06	16.0
Clothing	188.50	13.6
Leisure time	89.54	6.5
House operation	78.74	5.7
Investments	66.81	4.8
Automobile	41.26	3.0
Furnishings	36.42	2.6
Care of the person	34.42	2.5
Medical care	28.51	2.1
Transportation	25.78	1.9
Charity	14.31	1.0
Education	8.34	0.6
Associations	3.57	0.3
Other items	38.84	2.8